THE TEXT OF THE
NEW TESTAMENT

THE TEXT OF THE
NEW TESTAMENT

From Manuscript to Modern Edition

J. HAROLD GREENLEE

HENDRICKSON
PUBLISHERS

The Text of the New Testament: From Manuscript to Modern Edition
© 2008 by Hendrickson Publishers, Inc.
P. O. Box 3473
Peabody, Massachusetts 01961-3473

ISBN 1-978-59856-240-8

The book is a revision and expansion of *Scribes, Scrolls, and Scripture* (Grand Rapids: Eerdmans, 1985).

The Nomina Sacra, SymbolGreekII, and Uncial fonts used in this work are available from Linguist's Software, Inc., PO Box 580, Edmonds, WA 98020-0580 USA tel (425)775-1130 www.linguistsoftware.com.

Printed in the United States of America

Second Printing—May 2009

The Codex Purpureus Rossanensis, a 6th century manuscript on purple parchment, is one of the oldest surviving illuminated manuscripts of the New Testament. It contains the Gospel of Matthew and almost the entire Gospel of Mark. 30 x 25 cm. Inscriptions and 40 verses are from Psalms and Prophets. Folio 45: the Gospel of Matthew. The writing is silver with extra large, square letters called "biblical capital." Origin perhaps Aleppo, Syria.
Location: Biblioteca Arcivescovile, Rossano, Italy
Photo Credit : Erich Lessing / Art Resource, N.Y.

Library of Congress Cataloging-in-Publication Data

Greenlee, J. Harold (Jacob Harold), 1918–
    The text of the New Testament : from manuscript to modern edition / J. Harold Greenlee. — Revision and expansion.
      p. cm.
    Rev. ed. of: Scribes, scrolls, and scripture.
    Includes bibliographical references (p.   ) and indexes.
    ISBN 978-1-59856-240-8 (alk. paper)
    1. Bible. N.T.—Criticism, Textual. I. Greenlee, J. Harold (Jacob Harold), 1918– Scribes, scrolls, and scripture. II. Title.
    BS2325.G68 2008
    225.4'86—dc22

2008005382

To my wife Ruth and
my children Dorothy, Lois, and David

Contents

Preface

Today, as in the past, the average Christian who loves and reads the New Testament is sadly uninformed about the background and history of this most important book. He or she tends to think of it as an English book. He or she also tends to think of it as speaking a special form of English; many Christians still feel a bit uneasy about a Bible that does not sound a bit ancient. Indeed, the King James Version of the Bible (KJV), surely one of the masterpieces of English literature, was the Bible for English readers for so many generations that this translation is often regarded as the "real" Bible, to which any other version should be compared for approval.

Yet the New Testament is a Greek book—or rather a collection of books—written by several authors under the inspiration of the Holy Spirit over nineteen hundred years ago, and written in the kind of Greek that ordinary people spoke every day. Well over a thousand years passed before it was translated into English; it had been translated into many other languages before John Wycliffe first put it into the language of the British peasant. Several subsequent English translations were made before the version authorized by King James of England was published less than four hundred years ago.

Of course, the most important thing is to believe and obey the New Testament, not merely to know the story of its origin. Yet this lack of acquaintance with the history of the New Testament as we have it today has led to misunderstanding and confusion. Some voices are proclaiming that many or all of the recent English translations of the New Testament are corrupted, or are translated from corrupted and heretical ancient manuscripts (MSS), and that the KJV and the Greek MSS from which it was translated are the only pure and reliable forms of the New Testament.

How were the books of the New Testament originally written? Can we be sure that the true text of the New Testament has survived in any form after all these centuries? What must we think about the multitude of differences between the ancient MSS? Did some ancient scribes intentionally "water down" or corrupt the New Testament text as they were copying it? Do modern English translations adequately preserve the message of the ancient writers? These are questions that should be of concern to the sincere Christian; these are some of the questions this book attempts to answer in layman's language but with scholarly accuracy.

It is my hope and prayer that this little volume will bring illumination to many people concerning God's word to people and encouragement to believe that this message has been preserved in the versions of the New Testament we read today.

A previous edition of this book was published under the title *Scribes, Scrolls, and Scripture*. The present edition has been updated to reflect some of the most recent developments related to the New Testament text and expanded to include important discussions among textual critics since the previous edition was published. I am grateful to Hendrickson Publishers for offering this new edition to the public, and specifically to Dr. Mark House for his work in updating the work, expanding the sixth through eighth chapters, and contributing a new ninth chapter. I also wish to thank Dr. Daniel Wallace for suggesting several corrections and additions to the manuscript prior to publication.

Abbreviations

A.D.	anno Domini (the year of our Lord)
B.C.	before Christ
cf.	compare
1 Chr	1 Chronicles
Cod.	Codex
Col	Colossians
1, 2 Cor	1, 2 Corinthians
e.g.	*exempli gratia*, for example
Eph	Ephesians
ESV	English Standard Version
Gal	Galatians
GNT	*Greek New Testament*
i.e.	*id est*, that is
ibid.	*ibidem*, in the same place
KJV	King James (Authorized) Version
LXX	Septuagint (Greek) translation of the Old Testament
Matt	Matthew
MS(S)	manuscript(s)
NA	Nestle-Aland Greek text
NEB	New English Bible
NIV	New International Version
NKJV	New King James Version
NLT	New Living Translation

NRSV	New Revised Standard Version
NTG	*Novum Testamentum Graece*
1, 2 Pet	1, 2 Peter
Phil	Philippians
REB	Revised English Bible
Rev	Revelation
Rom	Romans
TEV	Today's English Version
1, 2 Thess	1, 2 Thessalonians
1, 2 Tim	1, 2 Timothy
UBS	United Bible Societies
v.	verse

CHAPTER ONE

What Ancient Books Looked Like

What did a book of the New Testament look like when it was first written in the year A.D. 50, 60, 70, or some other date in the first Christian century? After the books were written, how were they copied and handed down through the centuries to reach us as we know them now? When we read our New Testament today, can we be sure that we are reading what Luke, John, Paul, and the other authors wrote so long ago? Why do various translations differ with one another? What about the footnotes that say, "Other ancient MSS read . . ."?

These are some of the questions that are answered in the study called "textual criticism."

From the most ancient times until just over five hundred years ago, when someone wrote a book, a poem, a letter, or anything else, there was no way of duplicating it except by hand, one copy at a time. Of course, most of the things that were written—letters, receipts, notices, and such—did not need to be copied. Among the other ancient writings, however, were great pieces of literature of which many people wanted copies, not only soon after they were written but for many centuries afterward. This was the situation with the Bible, too, of course. As a result of this demand, hundreds of ancient MSS (i.e., handwritten copies) not only of the biblical books but also of many of the books of other authors of ancient times can be seen today in libraries in many parts of the world. After an author wrote his book (the original MS was called an "autograph," meaning "self-writing"), his MS was copied, then copies were made from this copy, others from these, and so on, often through several centuries. The autographs of these ancient books, including the Bible, perished ages ago, and we have only copies of copies, most of them many copies away from the originals and therefore differing from the original and from one another to some extent.

It is because of this that the science of textual criticism is needed, for study not only of the Bible but of any ancient writing the original of which is lost. Textual criticism is the study of copies of an ancient writing to try to determine the exact words of the text as the author originally wrote them. Scholars use textual criticism to study the MSS of the classical authors, especially the Greek and Latin writers, such as Plato, Herodotus, Homer, Livy, Cicero, and Virgil. Since the Bible is the most important of ancient writings, textual criticism of the Bible, and especially of the New Testament, is the most important field of textual criticism. In this volume we will be concentrating on textual criticism of the New Testament.

It is important to note at the outset, however, that textual criticism is not at all the same thing as literary criticism, which is sometimes called "higher criticism." Literary criticism attempts to find out the sources underlying an author's work—that is, it tries to determine where he got his information. This "higher criticism" has often been applied to the Bible in a destructive way, and it has come to be looked down on by many evangelical Christians. But, as I say, textual criticism is quite distinct from literary criticism. Textual criticism simply takes the known MSS of the New Testament, studies the differences between them, and attempts by established principles to determine the exact wording of the New Testament originals.

The Importance of New Testament Textual Criticism

As I just noted, the most important field of textual criticism is the study of the MSS of the New Testament. This is true for three reasons. In the first place, the New Testament is the most important of all ancient literary works. In the second place, the number of ancient MSS of the New Testament known today is far greater than that of any other ancient book. This gives the New Testament a far greater field for the application of textual criticism. The ancient Greek and Latin classics are known today, in some cases, from only one surviving MS. In other cases there are three, fifty, or a hundred MSS. Homer's writings, which have some 2,200 MSS, are a rare exception. For the New Testament, on the other hand, we presently know of over 5,700 Greek MSS, 10,000 Latin MSS, and an additional 1,000 MSS in other ancient languages.

In the third place, the MSS of the New Testament that are known today include some that were copied much nearer to the time when these books were originally written than is the case with other ancient books. The oldest known MSS of some of the Greek classics were copied over a thousand years after the author wrote his book. The oldest known MSS of most of the Latin classics were copied from three hundred to seven hundred years after these books were originally written. In the case of the New Testament, however, one MS known today that contains most of the Gospel of John was copied less than one hundred years after the gospel was originally written, and we have numerous MSS of various parts of the New Testament that were copied three hundred years or less after the books were originally written.

What can we conclude from all this? If scholars believe the MSS of the classics at their disposal to be relatively reliable copies of these ancient books, how much more certain may we be, then, that the MSS of the New Testament that we possess give us the original text of the New Testament accurately, especially since there are so many more of these MSS, and since they were copied much nearer the dates when the originals were written!

We should also mention that MSS of the New Testament differ greatly in the amount of text they contain. One of the two oldest is a tiny fragment that contains only part of three or four verses of the Gospel of John. Other MSS contain the entire New Testament. Between these extremes, various MSS contain one New Testament book, one leaf, part of one book, or several books.

Although the many MSS of the New Testament differ from one another, we must not exaggerate the importance of the differences that are found in them. There is no question of separating "orthodox" MSS from "heretical" ones. In fact, all of the ancient MSS contain the word of God, and they all agree in most of the words of their text. Textual criticism, therefore, deals mostly with small details of differences between the MSS.

Why Textual Criticism Is Needed

Perhaps we should speak a bit more specifically about why it is so important to study and compare the ancient MSS of the New Testament or of any other ancient book. As we have noted, in ancient times the only way to reproduce a book was to make one copy at a time by hand. This meant not only that copies of the New Testament were expensive but also that no two copies of a New Testament book would be completely identical. Small errors and differences would almost certainly creep in as a result of ordinary human frailty, differences in handwriting, and the fact that the Greek text was written without any breaks between words. When scribes made further copies of these copies, they might discover and correct some errors, but they would unwittingly reproduce most of the errors and add a few more of their own.

Thus, in general, the more copies by which a MS is removed from its original, the more it may differ from the original. At the same time, it must be emphasized once again that the total of these differences and errors affects only a small portion of the text, especially so far as differences of meaning are concerned. No essential truth or doctrine of

Scripture is placed in doubt by differences between the most reliable MSS. Yet the New Testament is of such supreme importance that it is well worth our while to study the MSS to make even small improvements in our knowledge and our assurance concerning the original words of the authors.

CHAPTER TWO

How Ancient Manuscripts Were Written

Down through the centuries, people have written on a great variety of materials. In ancient times these materials have included such diverse surfaces as the leaves and bark of trees, linen cloth, broken pieces of pottery (called "ostraca" or "potsherds"), walls of buildings, metal, and wooden tablets coated with wax.

Waxed Tablets

Waxed tablets were used by people of Greece and Rome before the Christian era. To make these tablets, a piece of wood was hollowed slightly and coated with wax, making something that looked a bit like a child's slate of more recent times. Writing was done with a pointed stick called a stylus, and the writing could be erased by smoothing the wax surface. These tablets were used for temporary writings and for personal correspondence. They were also used at times for legal documents, in which case two tablets would be placed face to face with the writing inside and fastened together with leather thongs run through holes at the edges of the tablets. In one of his writings St. Augustine mentions some tablets he owned, although his were made of ivory instead of wood. Luke 1:63 tells us that Zechariah, the father of John the Baptist, used a tablet, probably of this type (this is what is meant by the phrase "writing table" in the KJV), to write his son's name.

Papyrus

Of course waxed tablets were not suitable for long stories or for any other text that was meant to be read again and again. For literary works the ancient authors used papyrus, the material from which our word "paper" is derived. The oldest known papyrus fragment comes from Egypt and is said to have been written about 2400 B.C. It was the most common writing material in Greece in the fifth century B.C. It was

Waxed tablet

inexpensive and convenient and was used for literary works as well as for such things as letters, receipts, and business matters.

The papyrus plant is a reed that grew in swampy areas in the Nile River delta and a few other places in the Mediterranean world. (I personally first saw papyrus plants growing in San Jose, Costa Rica.) The plant had a triangular stalk (although I am told that those in the Los Angeles Arboretum have round stalks) with a tassel at the top, and grew to a height of six to twelve feet. In order to make writing material, the outer skin of the stalk was stripped off and the pithy center was cut into thin strips. The strips were laid side by side to the desired size and then another layer was laid crosswise on top. Either paste or the juice of the plant may have been used to hold the layers together. Once assembled, the sheets were pounded, dried, and then smoothed with a piece of ivory or a shell.

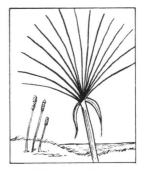

Papyrus plant

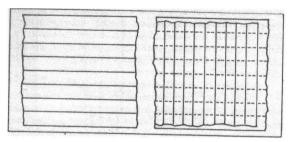

Papyrus manuscript construction: one layer of strips
was pasted crosswise over another layer.

The pith of the papyrus plant was called *biblos*, from which such English words as "bibliography" and "Bible" are derived. A papyrus sheet is mentioned in 2 John 12. The Greek word in this verse (*chartes*, from which the English word "chart" is derived) is translated "paper" in various English versions.

Papyrus sheets were made in sizes from about six by nine inches to twelve by fifteen inches. The sheets were overlapped slightly and pasted together in long strips of twenty sheets, then rolled up for sale. Of course, the purchaser could paste several rolls together if he wanted to produce a long text. The scroll of the Gospel of Matthew would have been about thirty feet long, which was about the practical limit for the length of a papyrus scroll.

During the time of the Roman Empire the government controlled the papyrus trade. As the rolls were prepared for sale, the names of the officials responsible for this trade would be written on the first page. The Greek term for this first page was *protokollon*, or "first glued sheet," and it is this word that has given us our English word "protocol."

A book written on these papyrus rolls was called a *biblos* or *biblion*. This word appears several times in the New Testament, including Matt 1:1, Luke 3:4, and Acts 1:20. It means "scroll" rather than "book" as we think of the term. If a book required several scrolls, each scroll or volume was called a *tomos*, which means "cutting." Even in our day a large, scholarly book is sometimes called a "weighty tome."

Writing was done on the side of the scroll on which the papyrus strips were laid horizontally, and the scroll was always rolled so that this would be the inside of the scroll. It was more difficult to write on the other side of the scroll, where the papyrus strips were laid vertically, because this entailed writing across the fibers of the papyrus. Only rarely was this done; however, Rev 5:1 refers to such a scroll written on both sides, prob-

Ancient scroll

ably to indicate that the author had so much to say that he could not get it all written on the proper side of the scroll.

The Egyptians exported papyrus rolls to other countries. Papyrus was the most common writing material until the third Christian century, and it continued to be used for secular classical literature until the sixth or seventh century. So it is clear that the original MSS of the New Testament were written on papyrus. Papyrus sheets were perishable, however, and few books or other documents written on papyrus in ancient times have survived except in a few very dry places, such as the sands of Egypt.

Parchment

The skins of animals, made into scrolls of tanned leather, were also used to receive writing in ancient times. Skins made strong and durable rolls. They were used by the Persians, the Greeks, and especially by the Hebrews, but not much by the Egyptians, since Egypt had a plentiful supply of papyrus. The oldest leather scroll presently known is one written in 1468 B.C. describing the victory by King Tuthmosis III at Megiddo in that year. The Hebrews continued to use leather scrolls for their Scriptures long into the Christian era, and even now leather scrolls of the Hebrew Old Testament are common in Jewish places of worship.

It was a later improvement, however, that brought animal skins into common use as a writing material. In this process, instead of being tanned, the skins were soaked in quicklime water, and the hair was scraped off. The skins were scraped on both sides, dried, and rubbed with chalk and pumice stone. The result was a fine, smooth writing surface of long-lasting quality.

Skins treated in this way were known as "vellum" or "parchment." *Vellum* properly means "calfskin" (the word "veal" is related to it), but the term was later applied to other skins of finer quality as well. The word "parchment" comes from the name of the city Pergamus, which was noted for the quality of parchment produced there. The term was originally used to denote skins of lesser quality than the finer vellum. Now, however, the two terms are commonly used interchangeably.

When we compare the writing surfaces of papyrus and parchment, it seems surprising that people at first considered parchment inferior to papyrus. Papyrus continued to be the "proper" material for literary works, while parchment was used for such things as business papers, notebooks, and the first drafts of an author's works. As time passed, however, parchment began to replace papyrus as the accepted material for a "book." This occurred partly because as the need for writing materials increased, the supply of papyrus was not sufficient. The fact that it was easier to write on parchment and the fact that parchment documents lasted much longer likely constituted an even greater influence in effecting the changeover. At any rate, by the fourth century of the Christian era, parchment had displaced papyrus as the most common writing material, although papyrus continued to be used for another three centuries for classical literature and occasionally for New Testament MSS.

The very earliest known MSS of the New Testament, those that come from the second and third centuries, are on papyrus. During the fourth century, however, scribes began copying the New Testament on parchment, and parchment was the material used for almost all New Testament MSS from that time until paper came into use a thousand years later.

Paper

The invention of paper is attributed to a Chinese man named Tsai Lun, in A.D. 89. The oldest existing specimens of Chinese paper, from the fourth century, are made of hemp or flax. Paper became known to the Arabs about the eighth century and was introduced into the Western world at the time of the Crusades. Paper came to be used for books in Europe in the twelfth century and had practically replaced parchment by the fifteenth century. This was a timely development, since the invention of the printing press soon afterward brought about a markedly increased demand for writing material that parchment could not have met.

Implements People Used for Writing

When someone wrote on a waxed tablet, as we have noted, he used a pointed stick, or stylus, much like the stylus that is used today for writing by hand on a mimeograph stencil. The other end of the stylus usually had a rounded knob, which was used for erasing and making corrections.

For writing on papyrus, a pen made from a reed (called a *kalamos* in Greek) was commonly used. It is this sort of pen that is referred to in 3 John 13, which mentions writing "with pen and ink." To make this type of pen, the stalk of a hollow reed was cut and allowed to dry a bit. Then one end was sharpened to a point with a sloping cut, and a slit was made extending up the stem about a quarter inch from the point. Pens of this type were flexible, which made them suitable for writing on the fibrous surface of papyrus. After being used for a time, the point would become frayed and need to be resharpened. Indeed, the very earliest reed pens now known were evidently made with a frayed end like a small brush; scribes began to use the pointed form about the third century before Christ. Although such a

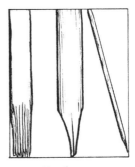

Reed pens

pen might seem to us to be a rather crude instrument, papyrus MSS demonstrate that a good scribe could produce beautiful writing with a good reed pen.

Quill pens

A different kind of pen is familiar to most of us from pictures we have seen representing people writing in past centuries—the quill pen. Quill pens came into use later than reed pens. They would have been too firm for satisfactory writing on papyrus, but they were well suited for parchment. The quill pen was formed by sharpening a goose feather to a point, much like a reed pen, but it lasted much longer than the reed pen.

In these days of ballpoint pens, we hardly give a thought to ink as a separate item. However, the older ones among us may remember the days of an ink bottle or an inkwell on the school desk and a pen with a steel point that had to be dipped into the ink after every few words. This is how writing was done with a reed or quill pen. Two kinds of ink were common in ancient times, and both can be seen in the MSS that have come down to us. One type of ink was made of lampblack (a substance like the carbon that collects on a dish held over a candle flame) and gum dissolved in water. This type of ink produced black writing. The other type was made from nut galls and produced a fine rusty brown writing. Red ink was often used for headings and initial letters, and other colors (even purple, gold, and silver) were sometimes used for special MSS. *Melas,* the Greek word for "black," is the word used for *ink* in 2 John 12 and 3 John 13, which probably indicates that black ink was the color most commonly used.

The well-equipped scribe's desk would include some other aids as well, such as a knife for making or repairing his pens, a whetstone for sharpening his knife, a bit of pumice stone for smoothing rough spots in his parchment sheets and for sharpening his pen point, and a sponge for erasing and wiping his pen.

"Books" in Ancient Times

The Scroll

The papyrus scroll books of the first century did not have an opening title page as we are accustomed to; rather, the title of the book was usually written at the end of the scroll. However, a papyrus tag containing the title was often attached to the scroll as an aid to the reader.

The columns of writing in a scroll were rather narrow, from two to three inches wide, so that the scroll would not have to be opened wide to be read. Space between the columns of writing was likewise narrow. The writing on a scroll was always done so that the scroll was held and opened horizontally, never vertically (in spite of the pictures so common on Christmas cards and the like, which mistakenly show someone holding a scroll open vertically). The scroll would be unrolled toward the left for Greek and Latin, which are written from left to right, and in the opposite direction for Hebrew, which is written from right to left. In some cases the scroll may have been rolled around a stick or roller (decorated rollers are quite common in Hebrew biblical scrolls), but more often the scroll was simply rolled on itself. When a reader or writer had completed a scroll, he would reroll it by holding it under his chin and rolling it with both hands. It was considered to be a mark of laziness if a reader failed to reroll his book when he had finished with it.

There are obvious disadvantages to a book in scroll form, as anyone who has attempted to locate a particular page in a long microfilm roll will attest. It was difficult to turn quickly to specific columns within a scroll, and if a reader wanted to interrupt his reading, there would be the question of whether he should reroll the scroll and unroll it again later or leave it opened in some safe place. There was even a proverb: "A great book, a great evil."

Papyrus scrolls are mentioned several times in the New Testament; references are usually translated as "book." Luke 4:17 speaks of the scroll (*biblion*) of the prophet Isaiah. John uses the same word to refer to his gospel in John 20:30. The "books" or "scrolls" mentioned in 2 Tim 4:13 may be either parchment scrolls or leather scrolls of the Old Testament. Rev 6:14 describes the sky as vanishing like "a scroll when it is rolled up."

The Codex

Although the scroll was the accepted form for a book in the first Christian century, there are no known surviving ancient MSS of the New Testament in scroll form. The early Christians often examined Old Testament passages to relate them to their faith, and looking up widely separated references in a scroll was a time-consuming task. A bit later, when some of the New Testament books had been written, the same problem arose in studying various parts of these books. As a result, when a form of book different from the scroll came into use, Christians were quick to see its advantages and began using this new form for their Scriptures when new copies were made. Indeed, scholars credit Christianity with exercising the greatest single influence in bringing about this change of book forms for works of literature. The new book form that replaced the scroll is basically the same as the book form we use today. The "codex" (plural "codices"), as it is called, takes its form from the ancient waxed tablets that were fastened together at one side with leather thongs as hinges. A codex was formed by laying several sheets— usually four—one on top of the other, folding them together, and then sewing them at the fold. This made a "quire." Then as many quires as were needed were bound together, as is done in modern books. In a papyrus codex, the sheets would be placed so that at any given opening both pages would have either horizontal or vertical strips. In parchment

Codex

quires, facing pages would be either the hair side or the flesh side of the skin.

From our idea of a book, it may seem strange that when the codex was first developed, it was regarded as a sort of notebook, to be used for letters, business papers, or for the first draft of an author's book or poems, and that the final "published" work would be in a scroll. As time passed, the advantages of the codex for works of literature became evident, however. Christians began to copy their Scriptures in codex MSS at an early date, although we cannot be sure exactly when. Since the Gospels and Acts were "books," it seems probable that they were initially written by their authors on papyrus scrolls. At the same time, scholars speculate that a problem involving the last twelve verses of Mark that we will investigate in a later chapter could have resulted from the loss of some text from the autograph or a very early copy. It would have been much easier to lose the final page or quire from a codex than to lose the last portion of a scroll, since the last portion of a scroll would normally be at the inside of the roll.

The epistles of the New Testament, on the other hand, with the possible exception of Hebrews, were not written as books but as letters to churches and individuals. These may therefore have been written originally on papyrus codices.

At any rate, even the oldest MSS of the New Testament known today do not take us back to a time when it was copied on scrolls. The oldest New Testament MS now known, as we mentioned earlier, is a small papyrus fragment in the Rylands Library of Manchester, England, dating from 100–150 A.D. and containing about four verses of John's gospel. It is clearly part of a codex, not a scroll, since the text is written on both sides of the papyrus. Nearly as old is a papyrus codex in the Bodmer Library of Geneva, Switzerland, dating from 150–200 A.D. and containing most of John. More than seventy other papyrus codices from the second, third, and fourth centuries are known today.

About the middle of the fourth century, scribes began copying on parchment. From that time, the parchment codex was the accepted form for New Testament MSS, although a number of papyrus codices from later centuries have come down to us.

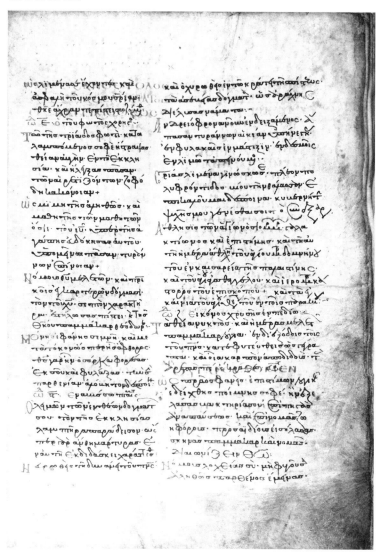

Codex 0209, a palimpsest MS dating from the seventh century. The earlier uncial text has been erased and written over with the fourteenth-century minuscule text of a Christian service book. Used with the permission of the Special Collection Library of the University of Michigan (Mich ms. 8, folio 110r).

In addition to the fact that a codex could be opened quickly at any point, this book form had another distinct advantage. The longest practical length for a scroll was about thirty feet. Using handwriting of ordinary size, a roll of this length could contain no more than one of the longer books of the New Testament, such as Matthew or Acts. A papyrus codex, on the other hand, could contain much more. Among the MSS of the Chester Beatty Library in Dublin, for example, is one papyrus codex that originally contained the four gospels and Acts, and another that contained the Pauline Epistles and Hebrews. With the further change from papyrus to parchment, it became possible to include the entire New Testament in one volume. Indeed, two of the most famous New Testament MSS, Codex Vaticanus of the Vatican Library and Codex Sinaiticus of the British Library, originally contained both the Old and New Testaments.

Since the supply of parchment was not inexhaustible, and the sheets were quite durable, when a parchment codex was no longer wanted, or if some of its pages had become damaged, the MS was sometimes taken apart, the damaged leaves were discarded, and the text was scraped off the usable leaves so that the text of a different MS could be written on them. A MS rewritten in this manner is called a "palimpsest," from two Greek words meaning "to scrape again." Even New Testament MSS were erased in this way. Indeed, more than fifty Greek New Testament palimpsests are known. Happily, the standards of erasing were not too high, and much of the text of these erased MSS can be read through and between the lines of the later text with patience, good eyes, and sometimes the help of a magnifying glass or scientific techniques involving the use of ultraviolet or infrared light.

The Handwriting in the Manuscripts

From before the beginning of the Christian era there were two kinds of Greek handwriting. One type is called "uncial" letters, which are a good deal like English capital letters in style, but rounded off to some extent and adapted for fairly rapid writing, although they were not connected. For many centuries uncial letters were the most common type of handwriting used in MSS of literary works, whether on papyrus scrolls, papyrus codices, or parchment codices.

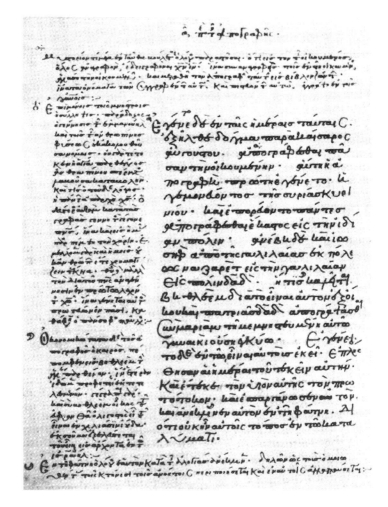

A minuscule MS, Codex 747, written in A.D. 1164. The larger writing, centered on the right, contains the biblical text of Luke 2:1–7. The smaller writing wrapped around it comprises writings from various church fathers. Used with the permission of Bibliothèque Nationale de France.

The words were written with no spaces between them, not to save space but simply as the accepted custom.

The other form of handwriting, known as "cursive," might be likened to a mixture of English longhand and lowercase printing, although the letters are less connected than they are in English longhand writing. This style of handwriting was used for personal and business writing such as letters and receipts. Cursive writing could be done much more quickly than uncial writing. Paul's letters to Timothy, Titus, and Philemon may have been written in cursive handwriting originally, since these were personal letters.

As time passed, it appears that scribes began to be interested in a more rapid way of copying MSS than was possible with uncial letters. Eventually, early in the ninth century, a new style of handwriting was developed. This new form of letters, called "minuscule," meaning "rather small," was a modification of cursive handwriting that was more formal and more legible than ordinary cursive. It was possible to write much more rapidly with minuscule letters than with uncial letters because of the form of the letters and the fact that some letters could be connected. One of the oldest minuscule New Testament MSS is a MS of the Gospels; it is the oldest known MS to contain a date based on the birth of Christ, as are our present calendars: it states that it was written in A.D. 835.

During the following century or so scribes began using the minuscule handwriting more and more in copying MSS, and by the end of the tenth century the period of uncial letters had come to an end. It can easily be remembered, therefore, that uncial MSS were produced in the eleventh century or earlier, and minuscule MSS were produced in the ninth century or later. About ninety percent of the known Greek New Testament MSS are minuscules.

Another general clue to the age of a MS is the fact that in both the uncial and minuscule periods the earlier MSS have little or no ornamentation, whereas the later MSS tend to have more decoration (often called "illumination"), in some cases including large ornamented initial letters at the opening of a book or the beginning of a new section.

Various contractions are found in MSS. The type that is most interesting is a special group of fifteen words called "sacred names" (the Latin term is *nomina sacra*) that are abbreviated by using the first one or two letters plus the last letter or letters of the word, with a horizontal line over the letters to indicate that it is an abbreviation. This group of words includes "God" (θ̄C̄), "Christ" (X̄C̄), "Jerusalem" (ῙΛΗΜ), and others.

CHAPTER THREE

The Ancient Records of the Greek New Testament

We have talked about how the ancient MSS were made and copied. We should now investigate these MSS as records in which the New Testament has been handed down to us through the centuries. How do we know today what the New Testament writers actually wrote back in the latter part of the first Christian century? What are the kinds of MSS in which the Scriptures were preserved until the invention of printing from movable type made it possible to make an unlimited number of identical copies of a book?

Greek Manuscripts

Autographs

The first group of MSS we should note is a group we don't have—the autographs, the original MSS of the New Testament books. Some authors may have penned their books them-selves; others may have dictated to a secretary, or "amanuen-sis." Some of Paul's letters indicate that he used an amanuensis. Romans 16:22, for example, reads, "I, Tertius, who wrote down this letter, greet you in the Lord." Second Thessalonians 3:17 reads, "I, Paul, write this greeting in my own hand, which is the distinguishing mark in all my letters. This is how I write," probably implying that someone else had written the rest of the letter at his dictation. First Corinthians 16:21, Gal 6:11, and Col 4: 18 have similar greetings from Paul said to have been produced in his own handwriting.

Papyri

The earliest MSS actually known to exist today are papyrus MSS in codex form. To date well over a hundred of these MSS have been discovered. Their contents and size vary from the tiny Rylands fragment we have already mentioned to codices that contain large portions of several New Testament books.

The first discovery of papyrus MSS in modern times was made in 1778, in the Fayum province of Egypt. More were found from time to time covered with sand or in rubbish heaps, preserved by the dry air of the region. Most of these papyri were nonliterary documents—receipts, personal letters, property deeds, and the like. For almost one hundred years their significance was not realized, and some were burned or destroyed in other ways. It was late in the nineteenth century when scholars began to realize that even these humble writings were actually treasures because of the light their contents shed on customs, ideas, culture, and the language of their times. A book entitled *Light from the Ancient East,* by Adolf Deissmann, gives a great deal of interesting information about these papyri.

A different and very important kind of treasure, however, was also found in these same rubbish heaps: works of ancient literature, both secular classics and biblical MSS, including some of the oldest MSS yet discovered of these writings.

Papyrus MSS of the New Testament have been discovered almost nowhere other than in Egypt.

For the purposes of textual criticism, all New Testament papyri are designated by 𝔓 followed by a number. The Rylands fragment of John, for instance, has been designated 𝔓[52]. The Chester Beatty Library collection in Dublin includes

$\mathfrak{P}^{37}$, a third-century Western papyrus MS containing the text of Matthew 26:19–52. Used with the permission of the University of Michigan Papyrus Collection (Inv. 1570, P.Mich. II, 137).

$\mathfrak{P}^{45}$ of the Gospels and Acts, $\mathfrak{P}^{46}$ of the Pauline Epistles, and $\mathfrak{P}^{47}$ of Revelation. $\mathfrak{P}^{66}$ is the Bodmer Library's papyrus of John. $\mathfrak{P}^{72}$, a third-century papyrus of Jude and 1 and 2 Peter, and $\mathfrak{P}^{74}$, a seventh-century papyrus of Acts and the Catholic Epistles (James; 1 and 2 Peter; 1, 2, and 3 John; and Jude), are also in the Bodmer Library. None of the books of any of the papyri is complete; many pages are damaged or missing in all of them.

Uncial Manuscripts

Although papyrus MSS of the New Testament are written in uncial letters, the term "uncial manuscript" is used to designate only *parchment* MSS written in uncial letters.

Although papyrus was still used for secular literature until about the seventh century, Christians began using parchment as early as the second century, and certainly by the third. By the time Emperor Constantine gave Christianity official recognition in the Roman Empire in A.D. 325, parchment was replacing papyrus as the dominant material used in the copying of biblical texts.

In recognizing the Christian religion, Constantine ensured that it would no longer be treated as an illegal and subversive movement. Christians were freed to worship openly and build church buildings. Moreover, the Christian Scriptures no longer had to be concealed for fear of confiscation, and copying them no longer had to be done in secret by people who were sincere Christians but were not professional and experienced scribes. Now the MSS of the New Testament could be copied openly and officially, although individual Christians continued to make their own copies as well. Indeed, in A.D. 331 the emperor himself ordered that fifty copies of the Bible be made for the churches of Constantinople, his capital city. In A.D. 350 some old and damaged papyrus codices in the famous library of Pamphilus in the city of Caesarea were replaced by parchment copies.

Parchment MSS have been found in many parts of Europe and the Middle East. A very few are now in the United States.

Codex Sinaiticus, a fourth-century uncial MS. This folio
contains John 21:1–35. © British Library Board. All
rights reserved (Add. 43725, f.260).

About two hundred years ago it became customary to
designate uncial MSS by capital letters. When all the English
letters had been used, the capital Greek letters that differ from
English letters were used. Even this addition yielded a total
of only thirty-seven letters, however, so the same letter was
sometimes used for two or more MSS that contained different
books of the New Testament; for example, one Codex D of the

Gospels and another Codex D of the Pauline Epistles. In 1844 the German scholar Constantin von Tischendorf discovered the MS now known as Codex Sinaiticus in the Monastery of St. Catherine on Mount Sinai. He was so impressed with this MS's importance that he did not want to have an insignificant letter assigned to it. Since the first letter of the English and Greek alphabets had already been used, he insisted on designating his new discovery by the first letter of the Hebrew alphabet, א (aleph), which has given headaches to writers and printers ever since!

As the number of uncial MSS coming to the attention of scholars increased, it became clear that a less limited type of designation was necessary. In 1890 Caspar René Gregory devised the system by which uncial MSS are now designated. Under this system uncial MSS are identified by a number prefixed by a zero (e.g., 02, 048, 0250). The MSS that were already identified by a letter, however, are still commonly referred to by their letter designation, even though they have been assigned an identifying number as well. Under this system, Codex Sinaiticus is Codex 01, which would have made Tischendorf happy.

Among the better-known uncial MSS are the following:

Codex Aleph (א, 01), Codex Sinaiticus, is now on display in the British Library. Written about A.D. 350, it originally contained the Old Testament, the New Testament, and some other Christian writings. This large MS (about 15 by 13½ inches) contains four columns of writing on each page. It is one of the most important MSS of the New Testament. It was taken from Mount Sinai by Tischendorf and presented to the czar of Russia. In 1933 the British government purchased it for about $500,000 that had been raised by private donations.

Codex A (02), Codex Alexandrinus, written in the fifth century, is on display beside Codex Sinaiticus in the British Library. It is named for the city of Alexandria, Egypt, where it resided before being presented to the king of England in 1627 by the patriarch of Constantinople. It originally contained both the Old and New Testaments, written two columns to the page in an attractive and more formal handwriting than that of Codex Sinaiticus.

Codex B (03), Codex Vaticanus, has rested in the Vatican Library for many centuries. Written about the middle of the fourth century, it is the most important single MS of the New Testament. This MS, too, contained both testaments, written three columns to the page.

Codex D (05), Codex Bezae (meaning "of Beza," because it once belonged to the scholar Theodore Beza), is a fifth-century MS that features Greek and Latin on facing pages. It contains the Gospels and Acts, written one column to the page. It is located in the library of Cambridge University. Another Codex D (06), Codex Claromontanus, containing the Pauline Epistles, is located in Paris.

Codex Ξ (the Greek letter Xi, 040), Codex Zacynthius, the Latin form of Zante, the Greek island from which it came), is an eighth-century palimpsest owned by the British and Foreign Bible Society in London. It originally contained only the Gospel of Luke, but it is unique in that it is the oldest known New Testament MS in which a very extensive commentary of quotations from various church fathers appears. This "catena," as the commentary is called, is written in smaller handwriting than the text of Luke, and in a different style of uncial letters. In the thirteenth century the MS was taken apart, damaged sheets were discarded, and the rest were erased. The sheets were then cut at the fold and refolded in the usual four-sheet quires to make a new book half the original size. The text of this later book is a "lectionary," a type of MS we will discuss shortly.

Codex N (022), Codex Purpureus Petropolitanus ("the Purple Manuscript of St. Petersburg"), together with Codices O (023) in Paris, Σ (Sigma) (042) in Italy, and Φ (Phi) (043) in Albania, are a group of four elegant MSS containing the Gospels written in silver ink on parchment dyed purple.

A good many MSS are, like Codex Sinaiticus, quite large, and many others are at least as large as a good-sized modern book in page dimensions. In addition to the MSS themselves, reproductions of various types have been made of a few of the more important MSS and can be seen at certain libraries.

Minuscule Manuscripts

A far larger group of New Testament MSS comprises those written in minuscule handwriting, dating from the ninth century to the invention of printing, and a few even later. Most minuscules are written on parchment, although some of the latest are written on paper. Like uncial MSS, the earlier minuscule MSS are generally more carefully written and have less ornamentation than those of later centuries.

Nearly 2,900 minuscule MSS are presently known to exist. They are designated by number (e.g., Cod. 23, Cod. 457, Cod. 2035).

Since most of the minuscules were copied later than the uncials, they are generally more copies removed from the originals than are most of the uncials and therefore may be expected to have more variations from the original text. This is not always the case, however. A twelfth-century MS might be only ten copies from the original while an eighth-century MS might be twenty copies from the original. Indeed, Codex 33, a ninth-century minuscule MS containing most of the New Testament, has such a reliable text that it has been called "Queen of the Cursives" (i.e., of the Minuscules). Codex 1, a twelfth-century MS, is probably the best MS of the half-dozen or so that were used to prepare the first Greek New Testament to be published after the invention of printing. Codex 565, in the public library of St. Petersburg, is one of the most beautiful of all New Testament MSS. Prepared for "the Empress Theodora," it is written in gold letters on purple parchment.

Lectionaries

Very early in the Christian era certain sections of the New Testament were selected for reading in services on each day of the year. Some New Testament MSS have indications in their margins of the beginnings and endings of these sections. Before long, however, these passages were assembled in the order in which they were to be read, and were copied in that order in MSS called "lectionaries," or lesson books. One type of lectionary contains a passage for every day of the year, beginning with Easter; the other type contains readings for Saturdays and Sundays only. Most of the passages are introduced by one of seven or so fixed phrases that fits the passage, such as "The Lord said to his disciples," "The Lord said," "At that time," and "Brothers." The majority of the lectionaries contain passages from the Gospels, but many contain passages from the epistles, and some include both gospels and epistles.

More than 2,400 lectionaries are known, the earliest consisting of fragmentary MSS from the fourth century written in uncial letters. Most, however, are from the minuscule period.

Lectionaries are designated by the letter "L" or the abbreviation "Lect." followed by a number (e.g., *l*225, Lect. 1280).

The number of known Greek MSS of all types amounts to more than 5,700, written from as early as the middle of the second century to as late as the end of the fifteenth century, and varying from part of one sheet to the entire New Testament. No other writing from ancient times equals the New Testament in the number of MSS that have survived to the present.

Even so, witnesses to the text of the New Testament do not stop with this mass of Greek MSS. Let us look further.

Versions

In ancient times, books were not usually translated from one language into another. In the few instances in which translation was done, the result was usually so loose and free a rendering that it would be of little use in determining the exact words of the original.

The first significant departure from this type of loose translation was in the translation of the Hebrew Old Testament into Greek over an extended period between about 250 and 150 B.C. According to a fanciful ancient tradition, the ruler of Egypt became interested in the Jewish religion and wanted to read the Jewish Scriptures, so he consulted with elders of the Jews and requested them to have a translation made into Greek. The elders then selected six scribes who knew Greek from each of the twelve Jewish tribes. Each of these seventy-two scribes was put into a separate room and assigned the task of translating the entire Old Testament. At the end of the allotted time of seventy-two days, the scribes were brought out, their translations were compared, and it was found that each of the seventy-two translations was identical to the others word for word! This gave confirmation to the Egyptian ruler that the Jewish Scriptures were surely from God.

Although this story is obviously unhistorical, the tradition does account for the name given to this translation. It is called the *Septuagint,* from the Latin word for "seventy" (shortened from "seventy-two" for convenience); it is often designated by the Roman numeral symbol for seventy, LXX. At least two other translations of the Old Testament into Greek were made, but the Septuagint is the best-known and is the translation to which the New Testament writers commonly referred when they quoted the Old Testament in the New Testament books. It is also the form of the Old Testament of Codices Sinaiticus and Vaticanus.

Almost as soon as the New Testament books were written, the gospel was being preached to people of other languages, and there was consequently a need to translate the New Testament into these languages. The translations that were produced have likewise come down to us in the form of ancient MSS. These translations, or versions, were faithful renderings, and they are therefore useful to us in textual criticism of the New Testament. Of course the value of a version for textual criticism is not so much the text of the version itself as the light that it sheds on the Greek text from which the version is translated. In addition, since the approximate date when the version was made is usually known, as is the general geographic area or country in which it was made, the versions give us helpful information about the particular form of the Greek text that was read and known in that location at that period of time.

Since Latin was the language of Rome, a Latin translation of the New Testament was needed very early in the missionary work of the young Christian church. It is likely that several translations into Latin were made before the end of the second century, because the surviving MSS differ from one another almost too much to have come from a single original translation. This early Latin is known as the Old Latin, or the Itala. The MSS of the Old Latin that have come down to us indicate that this version was used at least to some extent until the ninth century or later.

As the Roman church became more important, and particularly after Christianity gained official status in the Roman Empire, the Latin New Testament became more important, and the variety of readings in the Old Latin MS became more troublesome. Finally in A.D. 382 Pope Damasus commissioned Jerome, the outstanding Bible scholar of the day, to revise the Latin Bible to make it agree with the Greek text more closely. With the later help of other scholars, this new Latin version was completed after some years. It became known as the Latin Vulgate, meaning the "common Latin" version, and to this day it remains the official version of the Roman Catholic Church.

The Latin Vulgate was a translation that could be understood by the ordinary people who spoke Latin. Yet as time passed and the Latin language changed and other languages developed from it, the Latin Vulgate Bible was not altered or revised. Within a few centuries, this version that had been made to enable ordinary people to read the Bible had become a book that only priests and scholars could understand. The church authorities, moreover, were by that time declaring that it was dangerous for the lay people to read the Scriptures, lest they develop heretical ideas from them.

The influence of the Latin Vulgate is indicated by the fact that about ten thousand MSS of the Vulgate New Testament are known today, more than all the known Greek New Testament MSS of every type combined. This great number, coming from every century from the fifth to the fifteenth, reflects the fact that for many centuries the Bible of the Christian church was the Latin Bible. During much of this period, Greek was little known and its importance little recognized outside of Greece.

Syriac, a language closely related to the Aramaic that Jesus and his disciples spoke, was the language of some of the countries neighboring Palestine. Syriac, too, needed a translation of the New Testament in the very early days of the Christian church. It is possible that the Gospels were first translated from the Greek original into Syriac during the middle of the second century in the form of the *Diatessaron* (meaning "through the four"), a version that sought to combine all four gospels into one continuous account. This work is credited to a man named Tatian, but we have little direct knowledge of it.

The New Testament was probably translated into Syriac during the second century. Two MSS of parts of the New Testament in this Old Syriac, as it is called, are known today. A Syriac version called the *Peshitto* (meaning "simple"), which is still the recognized Syriac New Testament, was made about the beginning of the fifth century. The Peshitto did not contain 2 Peter, 2 or 3 John, Jude, or Revelation, since the Syriac church did not at that time accept these books as canonical (i.e., as part of the inspired New Testament text). These books were later supplied from subsequent Syriac translations called the *Philoxenian* and the *Harkleian*.

During the past few years some individuals have made much of the fact that Syriac is closely related to Aramaic. Claims have been made that the Syriac New Testament is the "genuine" New Testament, written in the language that Jesus spoke. One proponent of this view published a New Testament "from Eastern sources" and succeeded in impressing many people with its importance. More recently, a MS of the Syriac Peshitto was carried around the United States with great ceremony (one state governor took his oath of office with one hand on an English Bible and the other hand resting on this MS!) and with claims that the MS represented the New Testament in its original language. But even if Syriac and Aramaic were the same language—which they are not (for one thing, they were written with completely different alphabets)— the fact remains that the New Testament was originally written in Greek, and the New Testament in any language other than Greek is a translation from the original Greek and is thus one step removed from the original.

The gospel was carried to Egypt, too, at an early period, and the New Testament was translated into several dialects of the Egyptian language over an extended period of time. This language, called Coptic, was written in a combination of Greek letters and some additional symbols that were needed to indicate Coptic sounds that did not occur in Greek. A translation into the Sahidic dialect of Coptic, spoken in the southern part of Egypt, was made in the early third century; the translation into Bohairic, the dialect of Alexandria and the north, may not have been made until the fourth century.

Other early versions have some significance for New Testament textual criticism. One of these is Gothic, spoken by tribes near the Danube River in Europe; the New Testament was translated into Gothic by Bishop Ulfilas in the fourth century. The Armenian translation of the New Testament was made in the fifth century using an alphabet newly developed for this language by a monk named Mesrop. This same Mesrop is credited with developing a special alphabet for the translation of the New Testament into the Georgian language as well, which was spoken by the people of the region between the Black and Caspian Seas. Finally, the Slavonic version is credited to two brothers named Cyril and Methodius, who were missionaries during the ninth century in what is now Bulgaria. Cyril is credited with the invention of one form of the Slavic alphabet, which is called Cyrillic in his honor.

Of course, we do not have the original MSS, or even near originals, of any of these versions. In order to use these versions to help us know the Greek text from which they were made, we must first apply principles of textual criticism to the existing MSS of the version to determine as nearly as possible what the original text of the version was.

Patristic Quotations

The final major source of our knowledge of the text of the New Testament is the quotations of the New Testament found in the writings of the ancient Christian writers commonly called the church fathers. The writings are known as "patristic" (from *pater*, Latin for "father"). Most of the church fathers wrote in Greek or Latin, but some wrote in Syriac and a few other languages.

The New Testament quotations in these patristic writings are remarkably extensive. Indeed, it has been said that the whole New Testament could be reconstructed from these patristic quotations alone.

As in the case of the versions, we know when and where each of the church fathers lived, and so the form in which a father quoted a New Testament passage can show us the textual form in which the passage was known in a given location at a particular time. These references must be examined with special care, however, to determine whether the writer copied the quotation directly from a MS, recalled it from memory (in which case differences could be attributed to inaccuracies of memory rather than textual differences in a MS), or was making a reference or allusion that was not intended to be a direct quotation.

As with the versions, we do not have the original MSS of the fathers' writings, so principles of textual criticism must be applied to the later copies in order to determine as nearly as possible the exact form of the fathers' original writings and of the quotations contained in them.

Some of the more important Greek church fathers are Irenaeus, bishop of Lyons (second century); Clement of Alexandria (second and third centuries); Origen of Alexandria and later of Caesarea (third century); Eusebius Pamphili of Caesarea (fourth century); John Chrysostom ("John Golden-mouth," so named for his eloquence) of Constantinople (fourth century); and Cyril of Alexandria (fifth century). The Latin fathers include Tertullian (second and third centuries); Jerome (fourth and fifth centuries), who was responsible for the Latin Vulgate Bible; and Augustine (fourth and fifth centuries).

CHAPTER FOUR

The New Testament through the Centuries

We have looked into the way in which the New Testament books were written and noted the forms in which the New Testament has been preserved. Now let us take up the ways in which the MSS of the New Testament were copied and passed on through the centuries to bring the word of God to us.

This is a very important aspect of our study, because no matter how accurate the books of the New Testament may have been in their original form, we do not have these original MSS. What we know about the contents of the New Testament comes from copies many times removed from the original MSS, copies made at various times through many centuries. We should face the fact that if these copies do not furnish us with the true text of the New Testament, we have no way of knowing what the authors actually wrote, no matter how important their message may have been. It would be very dangerous to say as some people do that in certain passages the MSS agree but that the original text must have been different and was lost in the process of copying. Such proposals open the door to changing the scriptural text virtually anywhere it does not agree with the reader's prejudices. We must trust that the same Holy Spirit who inspired the original text was able to protect it through the centuries of hand-written copying.

As Christians, we believe that the Holy Spirit guided the authors of the New Testament books so that their message would be protected from error. As 2 Pet 1:21 puts it, "For prophecy never had its origin in the will of man, but men spoke from God as they were carried along by the Holy Spirit." We likewise believe that the Holy Spirit operated providentially in the copying and preservation of the MSS through the centuries. At the same time, we should not think that it was only by supernatural preservation that the New Testament was kept from being lost or hopelessly confused during those centuries. Many other ancient books were copied and recopied down through the years, and although some of them have been lost, many others have come down to us in reliable form. Even on merely human presuppositions there is no reason to believe that the New Testament as we have it today is not essentially reliable, accurately representing the original text.

Although the process of copying ancient MSS was basically the same for the New Testament as for secular literature, there were nevertheless some differences, especially during the two and a half centuries before Christianity gained official recognition in the Roman Empire. The secular classics were usually, though not always, copied by professional scribes and checked against accepted copies or originals by professional proofreaders. The New Testament, on the other hand, was probably copied during this earliest period mostly by ordinary Christians who were not professional scribes but who wanted a copy of a New Testament book or books for themselves or for other Christians. They did not have the same opportunity as the secular copyists to compare their MSS with other MSS because of the persecution that was often near at hand and that kept them from displaying their Scriptures too openly. In addition, copying a book by hand was a slow and tedious task; probably very few early Christian families possessed an entire New Testament.

As we noted earlier, hand copying a MS of more than two or three pages, no matter what its text, will almost certainly involve making some changes from the original. This is all the more likely to be true in Greek texts, in which no spaces are inserted between the words. As a result, probably no two MSS of a New Testament book or any other ancient book are absolutely identical in words, spelling, and other details. Moreover, as scribes copied these copies, and other scribes copied their copies, they continued to make changes through the centuries. Most of these changes were insignificant; those that were of importance—the ones with which we are concerned—were introduced during the first two centuries after the New Testament was written.

This being the case, how can we be confident that the New Testament has been faithfully preserved for us? Some years ago a popular magazine published an article proclaiming that New Testament scholars admitted that the New Testament as we know it today may contain as many as fifty thousand errors. The author of the article considered this high number of errors as strong evidence that the biblical text as we have it is unreliable. Scholars today consider the actual number of differences between all NT manuscripts to be as high as four hundred thousand. However, what is at stake is not the number of differences, but their *nature*.

Let us look more closely at this great number of differences between the MSS. One of the largest groups of these "variants," as they are called, includes differences or errors in spelling. For example, the common Greek spelling of "John" uses a double *n*, but one good MS spells it with a single *n*. Differences like these are of no significance for meaning, and we can disregard them.

A second very large group of variants involves other changes in the Greek text that make no difference in meaning. Many of them entail differences in the Greek for which there is no real counterpart in the English language. For example, in Greek a person's name can be written either with or without the Greek equivalent of "the" preceding it, whereas in English we do not say anything like "the Andrew saw the Jesus." As another example, in Greek the phrase "the good man" can also be written "the man the good," but in English both phrases could only be translated as "the good man."

A third type of variant is less common, involving instances in which the scribe accidentally makes nonsense of a phrase or writes a word that is clearly incorrect. Copying Luke 6:41, for example, one scribe accidentally wrote the Greek letter *pi* instead of *phi,* making the verse read "Let me take the *fruit* out of your eye" instead of "Let me take the *speck* out of your eye"! As a more recent example of such a blunder, I have a copy of an early edition of the "Good News for Modern Man" New Testament (TEV) in which the entire last chapter of 2 Peter is omitted and "Philippians" is misspelled at the top of every page of that epistle!

The textual variants that concern us, of course, are those that affect the meaning of the New Testament in some way. There are far fewer of these, but we should be clear on the fact that they affect only a small portion of the New Testament text. If twenty MSS of a book of the New Testament were selected at random and distributed to twenty people who could read them, any person in the group could read from his MS and the others would have no trouble in following him in their MSS. Indeed, the verbal agreement between the various New Testament MSS is actually closer than the verbal agreement between many English versions of the New Testament.

As we look at the textual variants that affect the meaning of the text to some extent, we will find that some are fairly important while others are less so. In addition, for some variants it is easy to decide which is the correct reading, while in other instances it is very difficult. However, in no case does a central truth of Scripture or Christian doctrine rest solely on a disputed text.

In dealing with these variants, both the important and the less important ones, there are principles to guide us in making our decisions. We will be discussing these in a later chapter. These principles do not give absolute answers for every variant, but when they are properly applied, they reduce the amount of the New Testament text that remains in serious doubt and is of real significance for meaning to something less than an average of one word in a thousand.

The Development of "Families" of Manuscripts

Since copying MSS by hand tends to bring errors and changes into the copies, the New Testament books came to differ more and more among themselves as they were copied and recopied. This divergence was not merely random, however; rather, it resulted in a kind of grouping of the MSS into families or, as they are sometimes called, "text-types." Nor do we mean to imply that the divergences continued to accumulate so that later MSS become quite unreliable. Rather, the introduction of textual variants soon reached its maximum, after which additional errors and differences were largely attributable to a given scribe working on one or a few MSS.

Let us now look into how the families of MSS, or text-types, arose. Keeping in mind that this explanation is oversimplified, let us suppose that four copies are made from an original MS and that each of these copies has its own distinctive differences from the original. As further copies are made from each of the four, each further copy will contain most of the peculiarities of the copy that preceded it, although scribes might notice and correct some of the changes. In this way the copies made from each of the four will tend to be more like the other MSS of their "family" than like the MSS copied from any of the other three initial copies. All of them will contain the same basic text, but the MSS of each of the four families will share distinctive readings in which they differ from the MSS of the other three families. In addition, within each of the four families the MSS that are nearer to each other in the process of copying will be even more similar to one another. In other words, it is somewhat like the human race, in which all people look alike in general but each racial group has its own distinctive features, and close human relatives tend to resemble each other even more closely.

Although we cannot be certain of some details, it appears that at a very early date after the New Testament was written, some copies were multiplied in Palestine and other MSS were taken to various regions, including Alexandria, Constantinople, and Rome. In each of these localities further copies of the MSS were made. These copies contained readings distinctive of these groups and differing from the MSS produced in other localities, although all MSS agreed except in these details. Initially, textual scholars identified four principle groups of MSS, or text-types: the *Alexandrian,* the *Byzantine* (for Byzantium, another name for Constantinople), the *Western* (for Rome), and the *Caesarean* (for the city of Caesarea in Palestine). Some textual scholars have disputed the existence of a separate Caesarean text-type, which is characterized largely by a mixture of Alexandrian and Western readings that occur in a small group of MSS in the Gospels. However, most agree that Caesarean readings are valuable witnesses in their own right. In addition, there are numerous MSS and a few versions that cannot be classified as belonging to any of these groups. In general this situation was established by the time Christianity gained official recognition by the Roman emperor in the early part of the fourth century.

With the official recognition of the Christian religion by Emperor Constantine there came a new freedom to copy and compare MSS of the Bible on a more professional basis. As MSS were compared more freely, and especially as MSS from various geographical regions were compared, Christians began to realize that there were differences among them. This evidently led to some attempts to bring the MSS into greater agreement by making changes in the existing MSS themselves or by making changes as the MSS were copied. This was not done in any really thorough manner, however, nor by following any well-developed principles. It appears that preference was often given to the readings of Constantinople, since that city was then the center of the Greek-speaking church. This process of making changes and corrections continued for perhaps three centuries or so, with the result that the readings characteristic of Constantinople (the Byzantine readings) became the generally accepted form of the biblical text, and the readings characteristic of other regions were largely neglected. Of the MSS that are now known, almost all of those from the eighth century and later are Byzantine in their readings, and these comprise between eighty and ninety percent of all presently known MSS.

The statistics do not mean that the Byzantine MSS, or the Byzantine text-type, are either more correct or less correct than the MSS of other text-types, any more than the facial features of a family of ten children who resemble one another are more "correct" than those of a family of only one child. Indeed, if the number of known MSS were the deciding factor in determining the preferred text, we would have to follow the Latin Vulgate, for there are more known MSS of that version than of all the Greek MSS of all four text-types together. Our decision concerning the merits of each text-type will have to await our discussion of the guiding principles we must follow.

CHAPTER FIVE

The New Testament Meets the Printing Press

In the middle of the fifteenth century an event occurred in Europe that revolutionized the Western world of literature. In 1454, in the German city of Mainz, Johannes Gutenberg invented a method of printing from movable type. With this invention it became possible for the first time to print any number of identical copies of a book or other document and to print them with a rapidity beyond comparison with the snail's pace of hand copying.

In China it is claimed that printing from movable type has been carried on in that country since A.D. 1041, with the invention credited to a man named Pi Sheng. Because of China's isolation from the Western world, however, this development had no influence in Europe. It was only through Gutenberg's genius that this remarkable process was made available in the West. Its significance for our civilization is almost beyond comprehension.

As the printing press of Gutenberg and his partner Fust was followed by more and more such presses across Europe, the age of MSS, in their literal meaning of "handwritten" copies, drew to an end. Not every scribe immediately laid down his pen and joined the ranks of the unemployed or learned to set up printer's type, of course. Some hand copying continued for many years. Yet the invention of printing from movable type, which we take so completely for granted, marked the beginning of a new age, an age in which the distribution of books was no longer dependent upon copies tediously produced one at a time with no two copies exactly alike—an age in which the very possession of books would no longer be the virtual monopoly of the wealthy.

The first item that came from the press of Fust and Gutenberg was an ecclesiastical indulgence, a single-sheet document produced for Roman Catholic church authorities. The first Bible was produced two years later, in 1456. This first of all "first editions" was a Latin Vulgate Bible, since at that time scholars had very little knowledge of the Greek text, and the Vulgate was the Bible of the church. This edition, now known as the Gutenberg Bible, was a beautiful edition of "folio" size—about sixteen inches in height and twelve inches in width. About forty copies are known to be in existence today.

It took more than half a century before the Greek New Testament was printed, and it involved the very earliest example of lively competition in the publishing industry. In 1502 the Roman Catholic Cardinal Ximenes of Toledo, Spain, began to prepare an edition of the Greek Bible. He arranged to have the Old Testament printed with the Hebrew, Latin, and Greek texts in parallel columns. The Latin text was to be placed in the center column, the cardinal's editors stated, "just as Jesus hung on the cross between two thieves"! The New Testament had the Latin and Greek texts in parallel columns.

The New Testament of the cardinal's edition was actually off the press and ready for distribution in 1514, but the decision was made not to publish it—that is, not to make it available to the public—until the Old Testament volumes were ready. When the Old Testament was printed, publication was further delayed until the pope gave the necessary approval. Although this approval came in 1520, the books were apparently not actually available for sale until 1522. This Bible came to be known as the Complutensian Polyglot, *Compluturn* being the Latin name for the city of Alcala, where it was produced, and *polyglot* meaning "many tongues," referring to the three languages of the text.

Cardinal Ximenes' edition was thus the first Greek New Testament to be printed. But it was not the first to be published and placed on the market. A Swiss printer named Froben, a Protestant, heard of the cardinal's project and promptly sought out the scholar Desiderius Erasmus to ask him to prepare an edition of the Greek New Testament as quickly as possible. Erasmus had been anxious to publish a Greek New Testament and readily accepted Froben's proposal.

Froben made his request in April 1515. In July Erasmus went to Basel, Switzerland, hoping to find Greek MSS in a library there that would be good enough for the printer to use in setting up the type for publication of the text. He could not find a MS containing the entire New Testament, so he used about half a dozen MSS of various books of the New Testament. Where more than one of his MSS contained the same part of the New Testament, he made some comparison of their readings and made some changes here and there where he felt it was necessary. For the book of Revelation, Erasmus had only one MS. This MS had lost its final leaf, which contained the last six verses of the book, and in other passages the biblical text was confused with a commentary on the text that was intertwined with it. In these verses Erasmus simply made up his own Greek text, translating it from the Latin. As a result, some words in his text of Revelation have not been found in more than one or two Greek Greek MSS that were obviously made to order!

As quickly as possible, Erasmus presented his New Testament text to Froben, who hastened to set it in type and get it into the press. The edition was completed and placed on the market early in March 1516, less than a year after the project was initiated.

This first edition of Erasmus's Greek New Testament, a large folio volume of about a thousand pages, did not contain the reference to the "heavenly witnesses" in 1 John 5:7–8. His Greek text read:

> For there are three that testify: the Spirit, the water and the blood; and the three are in agreement.

Beginning about A.D. 800, however, some MSS of the Latin Vulgate had read:

> For there are three that testify in heaven, the Father, the Word, and the Holy Spirit, and these three are one. And there are three that testify on earth, the spirit, and the water, and the blood; and these three are in agreement.

As a result of this difference between the texts, one of the Catholic editors of the Complutensian Polyglot criticized Erasmus for omitting this reference to the heavenly witnesses, which of course is a strong affirmation of the Trinity. Erasmus responded that the passage was not contained either in the Greek MSS he had used or in any Greek MS he had examined after preparing his text.

Not long afterward, a Greek MS was shown to him that did contain the passage. It is now known that the MS was prepared by a Franciscan friar in Oxford specifically for the purpose of showing it to Erasmus; he simply made a Greek translation from the Latin Bible and inserted it at the proper place in the Greek text.

Erasmus strongly suspected that he had been tricked, but he nevertheless inserted the heavenly witnesses in his third edition of 1522, with a footnote indicating his doubts about the MS that had been shown to him. In his fourth and subsequent editions he again omitted the passage. By a quirk of circumstances, however, it was Erasmus's third edition that proved to have the most lasting influence on other editions by other editors, and thus the reference to the heavenly witnesses, which is not found in any Greek New Testament MS produced earlier than the sixteenth century, came to be an accepted part of the Greek text and later found its way into the KJV in English. Incidentally, the MS that was used to twist Erasmus's arm is Codex 61, now located in the library at Trinity College in Dublin, Ireland.

When the Complutensian Polyglot finally became available in 1522, Erasmus examined it and realized that at some points its text was preferable to his own. Because of this, in his fourth edition of 1527 he adopted some readings from the Complutensian. Yet the Complutensian Polyglot never had the influence on editors of subsequent editions that the work of Erasmus did. This was partly because Erasmus had had the advantage of getting his edition on the market before the Complutensian and partly because his edition was less expensive and was printed in a more convenient form.

Other editors soon began publishing the Greek New Testament. Most of these editors consulted the text of Erasmus, and they often virtually reprinted it as their own, since there were no copyright laws to protect an author's work—and sometimes few scruples on the part of the publisher. As we noted earlier, it was Erasmus's third edition that these other editors most commonly used, even though his fourth edition contained numerous improvements.

One of these other editors was Robert Estienne, a member of a family of printers in Paris and later Geneva. Under the name Stephanus, the Latinized form of his family name, he published four editions of the Greek New Testament between 1546 and 1551. A noteworthy contribution of his fourth edition was the introduction of the verse numeration that we still use today. Our chapter divisions had been developed about 1205 by Stephen Langton, Archbishop of Canterbury.

Two members of the Elzevir family of Holland published seven editions of the Greek New Testament between 1624 and 1678. They, too, borrowed heavily from the text of Erasmus. Among other features of their editions for which we are indebted to the Elzevirs is the phrase "Textus Receptus," or "Received Text," the phrase commonly used to refer to the Greek text of Erasmus and his followers. This phrase was first used by the Elzevirs in their second edition, published in 1633. In this edition they stated optimistically—in Latin, of course, as any good scholar did in their day—"You have therefore the text now received by all, in which we give nothing altered or corrupt."

In any case, we should note that this Greek text of Erasmus and the editors who followed him was by no means a precise text faithfully preserved from the original MSS of the New Testament. Rather, it was based largely on Erasmus's hasty comparison of a few MSS of no unusual value that he happened to find in the university library in Basel. He did have one tenth-century MS, Codex 1, which was older and had a better text than did his other MSS—but the fact that its text differed from that of his other MSS made him doubt its value, and so he did not make much use of it.

Of course Erasmus ought not to be blamed for his failure to appreciate the value of Codex 1, since neither he nor anyone else of his day had any understanding of the nature of textual variants and their significance or of the principles by which the correct readings can be determined.

The Textus Receptus did indeed become the generally received text for nearly three hundred years, as well as the basis for the translation of the early English versions, including the KJV, and various versions in other European languages. Despite its deficiencies, this text does not distort the essential New Testament message. Yet in numerous details it is not as close to the exact original text as are the best of the ancient MSS, and it is certainly inferior to the best text that can be determined by a proper comparison of the MSS using sound principles of procedure.

CHAPTER SIX

More Manuscripts, and What They Revealed

The publication of the Greek New Testament in multiple copies on the printing presses contributed to a renewed interest in the New Testament in its original language. This interest, in turn, stimulated the publication of still more editions of the Greek New Testament to satisfy the increased demand. Indeed, by 1633, little more than a century after the first edition was published, a hundred editions of the Greek New Testament had appeared, almost all of them closely following the texts of Erasmus and Stephanus. Gone was the day when a complete New Testament was the prized possession of only a few libraries, churches, and wealthy individuals. Now almost anyone who desired a copy could purchase one.

The Increasing Demand for a Better Text

This increased interest in the Greek New Testament now began to cause scholars to give attention to the many ancient MSS of the Greek New Testament that were to be found in the libraries of Great Britain, Europe, and the Middle East but that had lain neglected in the past.

As scholars began to give more attention to these MSS, studying and comparing them with the printed text, they came to see more and more that there were many differences among the MSS and between the MSS and the printed texts. They were forced to begin to evaluate these differences and to try to determine which MSS had the readings that were more likely the correct original text.

In the meantime, the printed text, since it was better known than the text of the MSS, came to be regarded by many people as the true original New Testament text, which therefore should not be tampered with. As scholars continued their work, however, more and more ancient MSS came to light and were examined, and more and more instances were found in which the readings of the MSS differed from the reading of the printed text. Some scholars became convinced that the Textus Receptus could be improved by replacing its text in numerous passages with readings from the MSS. Some even advocated setting aside the Textus Receptus altogether and making a new beginning based on a comparison of MSS.

Beginning early in the eighteenth century, new editions of the Greek New Testament began to be published, editions that were no longer simply reproductions of the text of Erasmus and Stephanus. One of the first of these was that of the English scholar John Mill. His edition, published in 1707, made only a few changes in the Textus Receptus. He did, however, make a significant contribution to the study of the text by including footnotes—which are now called a "critical apparatus"—containing many readings from seventy-eight MSS, some ancient versions, and a number of quotations from the church fathers. These notes made it easy for readers to see how these other sources differed from the Textus Receptus and to make comparisons for themselves. Even so, Mill was roundly criticized for tampering with the commonly accepted New Testament text.

In 1734, the German scholar J. A. Bengel published a Greek New Testament in which he made a few cautious changes in the Textus Receptus. In his critical apparatus he indicated additional readings that he believed were preferable to the leading of the Textus Receptus but that he did not actually put into his text. Another important contribution Bengel made was to classify the MSS he had studied into two groups based on the similarity of their textual variants. This grouping of related MSS was an important new concept in the study of the MSS.

Each MS is generally given a name or number based on the system of cataloging used in the library in which it is kept. A MS might be designated by a title such as "Papyrus Oxyrhynchus 2834," for example, or "Bibl. Nat. Gr. 222." It would be awkward to have to use such lengthy designations in a critical apparatus in which many MSS must be named repeatedly, however. To resolve the problem, in his 1751–52 edition of the Greek New Testament, J. J. Wetstein assigned a capital letter to each uncial MS and an Arabic number to each minuscule MS, as we noted in chapter 3. Wetstein then published a list that identified the MSS by the capital letter or number and by their local library identification. For example, the library designation for Codex B is Vat. Gr. 1209, for Codex 33 is Bibl. Nat. Gr. 14, for Codex 565 is Egerton 2785, and for Codex 225 is Vind. Suppl. Gr. 97.

Following the lead of Bengel and his classification of the MSS into two groups, other scholars moved away from treating each MS separately and toward arranging the various witnesses to the text—Greek MSS, versions, and quotations from the church fathers—into groups of texts that are closely related. J. S. Semler proceeded to identify three families instead of Bengel's two, calling them the Alexandrian, Western, and Eastern, reflecting to some extent the geographical areas in which he believed they had originated. Semler also listed a great number of textual variants in his editions, indicating the witnesses that supported each reading and giving his opinion as to which reading was the original text.

During this period, which extended from about 1633 to 1830, many MSS were read and collated. To "collate" a MS is to read it and compare its text with another text, normally a printed text that is generally available to other people (commonly the Textus Receptus), recording in a concise list the differences of the MS from the printed text. By using the collation together with the printed text, the reader could get the full text of the MS without having to consult the MS itself. And of course the collation makes clear where and how the MS differs from the printed text.

The Displacement of the Textus Receptus by the Eclectic Text

Although more and more evidence was being collected that indicated that the Textus Receptus needed to be improved and corrected at many points, it was not an easy matter to make the necessary changes. Very few people had any understanding of the MSS or the significance of the textual variants. Most people who knew anything about the Greek New Testament knew only the Textus Receptus, and many of these considered it to be the true original text that must not be altered—just as in our own day many people have loudly protested the publication of English New Testaments other than the KJV. The scholars who dared to make even a few changes from the Textus Receptus in their editions of the New Testament were severely criticized. Still, there was a continuing increase of evidence that the Textus Receptus did not fully represent the original text as the inspired authors had written it, and that the original text could be more nearly represented by substituting certain readings from other MSS. This evidence could not be ignored forever.

Finally, in 1831 a German scholar, Karl Lachmann, dared to publish an edition of the New Testament he prepared from his examination of MSS and variants, deciding in each case what he believed the original reading was, independently of the Textus Receptus. Unfortunately, he did not include in his edition any explanation of the principles he had followed in preparing his text, except to state that in a certain little-known theological journal he had written an article explaining his principles. He could hardly have succeeded better in opening himself and his text up to criticism! Lachmann was a Greek scholar, not a theologian, and so he may not have realized what strong feelings surrounded the Textus Receptus. At any rate, a few years later he published a second edition of his New Testament, this time with a full explanation of the principles he had followed in producing his text and in deciding between textual variants. His explanation finally silenced some of the criticism against his work and won support for his text.

An English scholar, Samuel Prideaux Tregelles, published a Greek New Testament during the period from 1857 to 1879 that was likewise independent of the Textus Receptus. He used fairly sound principles, which he explained clearly. His edition contained an extensive critical apparatus showing which MSS, versions, and patristic quotations supported his text in each instance in which he had chosen between two or more readings in the MSS. This clear presentation, together with his personal reputation and his recognized experience in working with the Greek MSS, helped to encourage acceptance of his edition.

One of the greatest names in New Testament textual studies is that of Constantin von Tischendorf. It would take a book to describe his career. Probably no other person has discovered and made known the text of as many Greek New Testament MSS as did this nineteenth-century scholar. In addition to many others, he read and published a text of an important palimpsest MS, Codex C, which is located in the National Library of Paris. The original New Testament text of this MS was written in the fifth century and then erased some years later to receive the text of some of the works of the ancient church father St. Ephrem. For this reason it is known as Codex Ephraemi Rescriptus, "the rewritten codex of Ephrem."

Far more significant was Tischendorf's discovery of the famous Codex Sinaiticus in the monastery of St. Catherine on Mount Sinai, the text of which he also published. Altogether Tischendorf made available to the world the text of more than forty MSS from libraries in various parts of Europe and the Middle East.

In addition to his MS studies, Tischendorf found time to publish no fewer than eight editions of the Greek New Testament between 1841 and 1872. His eighth edition consists of two volumes containing the New Testament text together with a vast and detailed critical apparatus, and one volume of extensive descriptions and identifications of MSS. The "eighth major edition," as it is called (to distinguish it from a one-volume condensation known as the eighth minor edition), contains an immense amount of information about MSS and their textual variants. Well over a century after it was published it is still a necessity for serious study of the MSS of the New Testament and their readings.

Tischendorf produced his eighth edition independently of the Textus Receptus. Its text is somewhat weakened by its heavy dependence on the readings of Codex Sinaiticus, which he had discovered a few years earlier, but the great and enduring value of this monumental work is its critical apparatus and its vast amount of information concerning MSS.

All of the editions we have noted had their influence in bringing people, little by little, to accept the fact that the Textus Receptus was simply one form of the Greek text and not necessarily the closest possible text to the original.

In 1881–82 one further edition of the Greek New Testament was published that climaxed the long struggle against the domination of the Textus Receptus. This edition brought general recognition of the principle that the original text of the New Testament should be determined by studying the many variants in the MSS and applying sound principles to make decisions. This watershed edition was the Greek New Testament published by two British scholars, Brooke Foss Westcott and Fenton John Anthony Hort. They spent twenty-eight years preparing the edition, which was published as a two-volume work, one volume containing the New Testament text and one volume entirely devoted to an explanation of the principles they had followed. Their text had an immediate practical effect: while they were preparing their Greek text, they made it available to the committee that was preparing the English Revised Version of the Bible, with the result that this English New Testament, which was published in 1881, includes many of their choices of readings rather than the Textus Receptus readings found in the KJV.

The principles that Westcott and Hort used and supported were not completely new, of course. They learned from the scholars whose work had preceded theirs, and they built on these foundations. Some aspects of their principles have subsequently been modified by many scholars. It is widely believed, for example, that they leaned too heavily on readings of the Codex Vaticanus (Cod. B) in their text. Nevertheless, on the whole their work remains a landmark in New Testament textual studies.

With the advent of the twentieth century, the focus of scholarly work on the text of the New Testament shifted back to Germany and the work of Eberhard Nestle and his son Erwin. In 1898 the elder Nestle published the first edition of his *Novum Testamentum Graece* (Latin for *Greek New Testament*, hereafter *NTG*), which was based on a comparison of the three most influential editions of the Greek New Testament of his time—Tischendorf, Westcott/Hort, and Weymouth. In each place where one of the editions differed from the other two, he recorded the variation in a footnote. As Nestle continued to correct and refine his work, his subsequent editions gradually began to supplant the Textus Receptus as the standard text used in churches and theological schools. The thirteenth edition (1927) of the *NTG*, edited by Erwin Nestle, included the first extensive critical apparatus that cited not only previous editions but also important individual Greek MSS.

In 1955, the American Bible Society, with the cooperation of several other Bible societies, initiated the formation of a committee of textual scholars to prepare for the publication of a new edition of the Greek New Testament geared especially to the needs of Bible translators and exegetes. Accordingly, the first edition of the United Bible Societies' (UBS) *Greek New Testament* (*GNT*) contained a critical apparatus that focused on the major textual variants of importance for translation and exegesis. The new edition also included a grading system by which variants were ranked (from A to D), based on the editors' degree of certainty as to the variant's authenticity.

In preparation for the twenty-fifth edition of the *NTG* (1963), Kurt Aland, along with his colleagues at the newly formed Institute for New Testament Textual Research, verified the readings cited in the critical apparatus against the original texts and expanded the apparatus with citations from many additional MSS. From that point forward the *NTG* began to be referred to popularly as the Nestle-Aland (NA) edition.

In 1975, the UBS Editorial Committee, responding to a host of recent MS and papyrus discoveries, completed the third edition of the *GNT*. That same year the UBS committee also became responsible for supervising ongoing editorial revisions to the *NTG*. In 1979, a twenty-sixth edition of the *NTG* was completed, incorporating fundamental revisions to both the text and apparatus and containing an identical text to that of the UBS third edition. Subsequent editions of both the UBS and NA New Testaments, containing the same Greek text but incorporating revisions in the critical apparatus, appeared in 1993. While the apparatus of the twenty-seventh edition of the NA *NTG* offers a wider selection of variants, the fourth edition of the UBS *GNT* focuses on a reduced number of important variants, citing the external evidence for each of these variants more extensively.

While the editors of the NA/UBS texts, building on the work of the nineteenth-century pioneers, continued the trend away from dependence on the Textus Receptus, they did not share the degree of confidence that Tischendorf or Westcott/Hort had in the Alexandrian MSS Sinaiticus and Vaticanus. Instead, using a method that has recently been referred to as "reasoned eclecticism," they weighed the variants of all three major text-types with a view to discovering which variant might have given rise to the others. They also sought corroboration from the internal evidence provided by the text itself, employing trusted criteria developed by their forebears. As a result of the careful work of the Institute for New Testament Textual Research and the UBS Editorial Committee, combining accurate data with well-established text-critical methods, the NA and UBS texts have become standard texts among scholars, translators, and clergymen.

While the form of the New Testament text has become more standardized in recent years, scholars continue to differ in their decisions concerning many textual variants in the MSS. Among many contemporary New Testament scholars, confidence in the Textus Receptus has been supplanted by confidence in the NA text. There are some, however, who continue to insist that not only is the Textus Receptus the best text, but that it alone is the word of God. As new MS discoveries are made, more texts are collated into electronic databases, and data is analyzed in more enlightening ways, our understanding of the history of the New Testament text will continue to grow. As our understanding increases, our grasp of the precise shape of the original text will also be strengthened.

In the meantime, it is important to see that the inspired, authoritative New Testament has come down through the centuries in a great multitude of ancient MSS that differ from one another in various, mostly minor details, that virtually all of these MSS give us the word of God, and that in the vast majority of cases, the exact wording of the original text can be confidently determined by studying the variants and applying sound text-critical principles to decide among them. In the next chapter we will look at the most important of these principles.

CHAPTER SEVEN

Determining the Correct Reading

We have noted that in hundreds of words and phrases of the New Testament the ancient MSS, the versions, and the quotations from the church fathers differ among themselves. In some instances there may be only two readings—that is, there may be only two choices of words. In other instances there are several readings, occasionally as many as eight or ten. Since this is the case, what hope is there that we can determine what the New Testament text actually is? How can we know what the inspired writers actually wrote?

In the first place, it is important to remember that even with the great number of variants, the MSS still agree in most of their text. In the second place, where there are variants, most of them do not affect the meaning of the text. Very few variants give meanings that are actually false, except for occasional scribal blunders found in one MS or a few; we will deal with these a bit later.

The reason for studying the MSS, then, is not to decide whether the New Testament does or does not teach certain basic truths but rather, for the most part, to decide small details and relatively minor matters. Someone might ask, then, why we should bother at all if no important truths are at stake. The answer is that the New Testament is of such supreme importance that if careful study will enable us to make our text even slightly closer to what the New Testament writers wrote, or if it will enable us to see that our New Testament is already as nearly identical with the original text as it can be made, it will be worth the effort.

Most people, of course, have no ability to study the Greek MSS and must simply accept one or more translations or versions in English or whatever their language is. This is quite proper. These readers are accepting the decisions of those who made the translation they are reading. Even these readers, however, will often wonder about differences they find between the various versions. How do we go about deciding between the differences in the MSS to determine which is most likely the original text?

Internal Evidence and the Basic Principle

The first and most basic principle of textual criticism is this: *The reading from which the other readings could most easily have developed is most likely the original.*

Let's look at one class of examples of this principle. In many passages in the Gospels, some MSS of one gospel agree almost word for word with another gospel, while other MSS differ somewhat. One such instance is found in the story of the rich young ruler. Mark 10:17–18 and Luke 18:18–19 agree in reading:

> "*Good* teacher, . . . what must I do to inherit eternal life?" "Why do you *call* me good?" Jesus answered. "No one is good—except *God* alone."

In Matt 19:16–17 some MSS are identical with Mark and Luke, while other MSS read:

> "Teacher, what *good thing* must I do to get eternal life?" "Why do you *ask me about what is good?*" Jesus replied. "There is *only One* who is good."

Which of these forms did Matthew write? Both forms are reasonable, and both are theologically acceptable. If Matthew originally wrote the form of the text that is identical with Mark and Luke, there is no apparent reason why a scribe should change it in a later MS. If, however, Matthew wrote the form that differs slightly in wording from Mark and Luke, a later scribe might easily have changed the text of Matthew to agree with the other two gospels. He might have done so unintentionally if the form in Mark and Luke were more familiar to him, or he might have done so intentionally to make Matthew agree more closely with the other two. We conclude, then, that the reading from which the other reading most likely originated is the reading that differs slightly from that of Mark and Luke.

To give another example, Mark 6:47 reads that the boat was "in the middle of the lake." In the parallel in Matt 14:24 some MSS read, "in the middle of the lake," while other MSS read, "a considerable distance from the land." The meaning of the two readings is essentially the same and no theological issue is involved. If Matthew originally had the same phrase as Mark, there would be no reason for a later scribe to change it; but if Matthew originally had the phrase that is slightly different from that in Mark, a scribe could have changed it to bring it into closer agreement with Mark. Once again, the reading in Matthew from which the other reading most likely arose and which is therefore surely the original, is the reading that differs slightly from Mark.

Scribal changes to make a passage of Scripture agree more closely with a parallel passage are called "harmonizations." This type of change occurs frequently in the Gospels, and most often the instances are the result of attempts to bring Matthew or Luke into closer harmony with Mark. A few instances, however, occur elsewhere, as in the similar passages of Eph 1:7 and Col 1:14. The Ephesian passage reads, "in whom we have the redemption through his blood, the forgiveness of trespasses, according to the riches of his grace." In the Colossian parallel most MSS read, "in whom we have the redemption, the forgiveness of sins," but a few MSS insert "through his blood," as in Ephesians. This phrase does have theological significance. It is included in both Ephesians and Colossians in the Textus Receptus and in the KJV, but it is not included in Colossians in most of the recent versions in English.

Did Paul include "through his blood" in Colossians as he did in Ephesians? Did a scribe add the phrase because he remembered the similar verse in Ephesians and thought Colossians was the same? Did a scribe deliberately omit the phrase from Colossians because he objected to the doctrine of the blood atonement?

Let's look at the last alternative first. The MSS that do *not* have "through his blood" in Col 1:14 read, "by making peace through his blood, shed on the cross," in 1:20 and include "through his blood" in Ephesians. Why should a scribe object to the mention of Christ's blood in one verse and not object to it a few verses later or in the parallel in Ephesians? We can conclude that the phrase was not omitted deliberately through theological prejudice.

Which form of Col 1:14, then, is most likely original? If the reference to the blood was originally in both epistles, there would be no apparent reason for a scribe to eliminate it from Colossians and leave it in Ephesians. On the other hand, if Paul did not include it in Colossians, a scribe could easily have added it later, either intentionally borrowing it from Ephesians or unintentionally confusing it with the Ephesian parallel and inserting it thinking that the phrase had been accidentally omitted from the MS he was copying.

We conclude, then, that Paul included the phrase "through his blood" in Eph 1:7 but that it was added by a later scribe in Col 1:14 and that translators should therefore not include the phrase in Colossians.

Should the presence of harmonizations raise doubts about the accuracy and inspiration of the New Testament, in particular the gospels, in which most of them occur? Not at all. For one thing, the gospels differ from one another on every page, even where there are no textual variants. To cite just one example, in Matt 15:28 Jesus says to the Syro-Phoenician woman, "Woman, you have great faith! Your request is granted," whereas in Mark 7:29 he says, "For such a reply, you may go; the demon has left your daughter." These differences merely reflect the fact that the Holy Spirit operated differently through each writer's personality rather than inspiring them all to express themselves in the same words.

This basic principle—namely, that the reading from which the other readings could most likely have developed is probably the correct reading—has some further implications. One of these implications is that in many instances *the more difficult reading is likely to be the original.* This statement needs to be qualified a bit, however. What we mean is that if one reading seems at first sight to be unexpected or difficult to understand, but on further study is seen to make good sense, then this reading is probably original.

Let us look, for example, at John 1:18. Many MSS read, "No one has seen God at any time; the only begotten [or *unique*] *Son,* who is in the bosom of the Father, He has declared him" (NKJV). Many good MSS, however, read, "God" instead of "Son." In the Greek MSS the difference between the two is a matter of only one letter. Either reading clearly refers to Jesus. The Textus Receptus reads, "Son," and certainly no scribe wishing to weaken the text would change it to the much stronger "God." "Only begotten Son" makes good sense, and a scribe would have no reason to change it to clarify it. On the other hand, "only begotten God" is unexpected and strange. For this reason, some interpreters who favor this reading interpret the word translated "only begotten" as independent from the word "God" and would thus translate the phrase, "the only begotten One, (who is really) God." Nonetheless, a scribe could easily have thought that the difficult phrase resulted from a mistaken repetition of "God" from the beginning of the verse and that if he changed "God" here to "Son," he would be correcting an error in the MS he was reading.

But can "God" be the correct reading here? Does it make sense that John would have written it? Yes, it does. Jesus is referred to as "God" elsewhere in the Gospel of John—in John 1:1, for example—and of course Jesus is called "only begotten" in John 3:16. If we accept the reading "God" here, the sense of the verse may be, as some interpreters have argued, "No one has ever seen God (the Father); the only begotten One, who is himself God (in his nature), who is in the bosom of the Father, has made the Father known to us."

This makes good sense and is in the spirit of much else in this gospel.

In this passage, then, the seemingly harder reading is preferable and is the reading from which the other reading could easily have developed.

Of course a "hard" reading is sometimes an obvious error. Readings of this type are usually found in only one or a few MSS. We noted earlier that the scribe of one MS accidentally changed "speck" to "fruit" in Luke 6:41. Another error of this type occurs in a variant reading of Mark 14:31, in which Peter boldly says to Jesus, "Even if I have to die with you, I will never disown you!" But one very old MS changes the order of one word and changes a Greek short *e* to a long *e*. As a result, this MS has Peter timidly saying, "If I do *not* have to die, I will never disown you"! Both of these examples are "harder readings," of course, but no great amount of study is required to see that they are merely scribal errors.

The principle of preferring the reading from which the other readings most likely arose has another corollary. This second application of the principle has two parts. The first part is that *the shorter reading is generally preferable* if the difference between the readings resulted from an *intentional* change by a scribe. The reason for this is that scribes of the earliest MSS occasionally added a word or a phrase to clarify a thought, but they rarely omitted words or phrases intentionally.

An example is found in the story of the Prodigal Son in Luke 15. In 15:18–19 the son says that he will say to his father, "Father, I have sinned against heaven and against you. I am no longer worthy to be called your son. Make me like one of your hired men." In some MSS, verse 21, in which he actually meets his father, includes the final sentence "Make me like one of your hired men," but other good MSS omit this final sentence. Which reading is correct?

If Luke did not include the additional sentence in verse 21, a later scribe could easily have done so. The scribe might have felt that since the son had said that he would say to his father, "Make me like one of your hired men," he must have said it. Or the scribe might have added it unthinkingly simply because it was included in verse 19. On the other hand, if this sentence was a part of the original text of verse 21, there is no apparent reason for a scribe to omit it, since it accords perfectly with the context. Someone might suggest that the scribe intentionally omitted this sentence in verse 21 because he felt it unnecessary to repeat everything that had appeared in verses 18–19. But study of the MSS indicates that scribes simply didn't work that way. The evidence suggests that the shorter reading is doubtless the original, even though good MSS include the longer reading.

The second part of the corollary is almost the reverse of the first. This part is that *the longer reading is often preferable* if the difference between the readings resulted from an *unintentional* or accidental change by a scribe. We know that scribes would occasionally skip a word, a phrase, or an entire line as they were copying. This type of error was particularly likely to occur when the same combination of letters appeared twice close together in a line or directly above or below in the line of the text being copied from. For example, 1 John 2:23 reads, "No one who denies the Son has the Father; whoever acknowledges the Son has the Father also." In the Greek text, the last three words in each part of the verse are "has the Father." Some MSS omit the entire second half of this verse; a scribe copying the passage obviously let his eye slip from the first "has the Father" to the second and omitted everything between the two phrases. Indeed, in the KJV the second half of this verse is in italics, indicating that this clause was not in the Greek text from which the KJV was translated. However, the clause is surely original.

Occasionally the opposite error will occur: a scribe will have let his eye skip back from the second occurrence of a word (or even a repeated letter or letters) to the first occurrence, with the result that the intervening words or letters will be written twice. I myself committed this error in English on one occasion; in trying to copy the words "Newberry Library" from a paper I was typing, I found I had written "Newberry Librerry Library."

In 1 Thess 2:7 the difference between the two readings "we were gentle" and "we were infants" is only the difference between one *n* and two. The question is whether there was originally one *n* and the scribe copied it twice or whether there were two and he overlooked the second one.

Although much of what we have just been discussing involves intentional changes, by far the most frequent changes are those a scribe made unintentionally. It is important to remember that the oldest Greek MSS were written in letters somewhat like capital letters and that words were run together without spacing. Consider the problems of reading page after page written something like this:

INTHEBEGINNINGWASTHEWORDANDTHEWORDWAS
WITHGODANDTHEWORDWASGODTHISONEWASINTH
EBEGINNINGWITHGOD.

In addition, with the differences between various scribes' styles of handwriting, several letters could be confused with one another, such as those in the following groups: ЄѲОС, ПГІТ, ΔΛΛ, and НН. The possibility of confusion was increased by the fibrous surface of a papyrus sheet or even irregularities in a parchment leaf.

An example of possible confusion of letters can be seen in 1 Tim 3:16, in which the difference between "God appeared" and "he who appeared" is merely two small horizontal lines: ѲС and ОС. In 2 Pet 1:21, the difference between "men spoke from God" in some MSS and "holy men of God spoke" in other MSS is only the difference between ПО and ГІОІ.

If a Greek MS was being translated into another language, such as Latin or Syriac, there are occasional passages in which the scribe could mentally divide the Greek words incorrectly and translate a different meaning from what the author intended. For example, the English sentence

ISAWABUNDANCEONTHETABLE

could be read either as "I saw abundance on the table" or "I saw a bun dance on the table." In Mark 10:40 Jesus says, "but to sit on My right hand and on My left is not Mine to give, but *it is for those* for whom it is prepared" (NKJV; italics indicate words not literally represented in the Greek text.)

Some ancient translators took the Greek letters *all ois*, "but *for whom* it is prepared," as one word, *allois*, "but *for others* it is prepared" (since there was no space between the original Greek letters).

A mistake in hearing could also lead to an unintentional error. This type of error could occur either if someone were reading a MS to a group of scribes as they copied or if a scribe were pronouncing the words to himself and forgot what the written form was. For example, in 1 Cor 13:3 the difference between "surrender my body to the flames" and "surrender my body that I may boast" is the difference between only two Greek letters that could easily be confused. As another instance, from very early times the Greek words for the plural pronouns *you* and *we* were pronounced alike. There are numerous confusions of these two words in the New Testament MSS, as in 1 John 1:4, in which some MSS and versions read, "your joy" and others read, "our joy."

At times a word is unintentionally changed to another word of similar appearance and meaning. In particular, a less common word may be changed to a more familiar word. For example, many English-speaking people reading the sentence "I know the man who is the vicegerent of the company" would say "viceregent" instead of "vicegerent." In Rev 1:5 the author doubtless originally wrote, "freed us from our sins." However, since he adds, "by his blood," which suggests washing, a scribe accidentally or intentionally added one letter to the middle of the Greek word, which changed it from "freed" to "washed." In this case the change was to a word of similar appearance rather than to a more familiar word. If the end of the verse had read, "by his cross," instead of "by his blood," the change probably would not have been made.

We see, then, that internal evidence is very important in deciding between differences in the readings of the MSS. At the same time, there are limits to the application of internal evidence. For one thing, scribes are human beings and do not always act in completely predictable ways. It is sometimes impossible to deduce how a certain variant developed or what the original reading is on the basis of internal evidence. Beyond this, scholars may differ both in their interpretation of how a variant developed and in their conclusions concerning the original reading.

Happily, there is an additional means for helping us to determine the original text of the New Testament that involves using the MSS themselves to aid in the decision. It is called "external evidence."

External Evidence

As we said earlier, three major groups of New Testament MSS, called text-types, have been identified—the Alexandrian, the Western, and the Byzantine. (A fourth, the Caesarean, has been identified in the Gospels, but is disputed by some textual scholars.) The MSS in each of these text-types agree with one another more closely than with the MSS of any other text-type and tend to share peculiar readings or errors. The situation is somewhat similar to the differences between the racial groups of humankind and the shared characteristics within each racial group.

At the same time, the MSS of a given text-type do not agree with one another completely. Within each text-type there are smaller groups that agree with one another still more closely. Even within these smaller groups no two MSS will be exactly identical. Here, too, the situation is analogous to that of subgroups and families within the races of humankind.

Sometimes a text-type will be divided on a particular variant, with its MSS supporting two different readings almost equally. Some MSS show a mixture of text-types, in some instances agreeing with one text-type and in other instances agreeing with another.

In order to use these groups of MSS to help us determine the original reading in variants, we will need to decide how reliable each text-type is, ranking them from most to least reliable. By "most reliable," we mean, of course, the text-type that most often seems to have the correct reading among textual variants. In making this determination, we will base our decisions on readings that appear in most of the representatives of that text-type, overlooking peculiar readings of only one or a few MSS of the group.

In order to determine the relative reliability of the text-types, we might examine a large number of variants (in a gospel, or in several epistles, or even in the entire New Testament), selecting only variants in which internal evidence points rather clearly to the correct reading. For each of these variants we could then note which text-type or text-types support that reading. The results of such an examination would reveal that the Alexandrian is generally the most reliable text-type, followed by the Western and Byzantine types.

Of course, no single text-type is always correct and none is always wrong, but such an examination gives us an additional basis for determining the original reading among textual variants. Other things being equal (although they often aren't!), we will usually trust the more reliable text-types over the less reliable ones. At the same time, we will usually favor a reading supported by more than one text-type over a reading supported by only one text-type. This means that at times we will have to choose between a reading supported by one good text-type and a reading supported by more than one less reliable text-type.

Since individual MSS are often relatively impure representatives of their text-type, sometimes text-types are divided in their support of particular variants. When this occurs, it is important to consider which MS witnesses support which reading. Which variant do the best representatives of the text-type in question (i.e., the oldest and most consistent representatives of that text-type) support? Making this kind of determination obviously requires a more detailed knowledge of the characteristics of individual MSS.

With this additional data we can return to an examination of variants with two basic questions to ask: first, "On the basis of internal evidence, which reading is the one from which the other reading or readings most likely developed?" and second, "On the basis of external evidence, which reading is supported by the most reliable text-type or combination of text-types?"

Armed now with both internal and external evidence, we can examine the variants with added confidence. In some instances, both internal and external evidence will support a reading—that is, it will be the reading from which the other readings most likely developed, and it will be found in the best text-types. In other instances, we will not be able to decide which reading gave rise to the others, but external evidence will clearly point to one reading. In still others, the MS evidence will be almost equally divided, but internal evidence will indicate fairly clearly which is the reading from which the others probably developed. Sometimes, unfortunately, internal and external evidence may seem to be contradictory, or neither will give a clear indication; in these instances a decision will have to be tentative and doubtful.

Now let's look at an example of each of these four situations.

In Matt 5:47 some MSS read, "Do not even pagans do that?" while other MSS read, "tax collectors" instead of "pagans." Considering first the internal evidence, the preceding verse reads, "Do not even the tax collectors do the same?" It is therefore likely that the correct reading in verse 47 is "pagans" and that a scribe changed it to "tax collectors" either unintentionally or to make it agree with the similar statement in the preceding verse. At the same time, there is no apparent reason for a scribe to have changed "tax collectors" to "pagans" here. Internal evidence therefore favors "pagans" as the original reading.

Looking at external (MS) evidence, "pagans" is supported by the most reliable text-type—the Alexandrian—along with the Western and some of the Caesarean witnesses; "tax collectors," on the other hand, is supported by the least reliable text-type, the Byzantine, along with other Caesarean witnesses. External evidence thus clearly supports "pagans." In this variant, then, both classes of evidence combine to support the same reading.

In John 5:44, in the phrase "the praise that comes from the only God," the word "God" is omitted in some MSS, giving the sense of "from the Only One" (which of course would still mean God). Looking at internal evidence, we note that in the Greek MSS "God" would have been written as ΘΥ in the following sequence of Greek uncial (capital) letters: ΤΟΥΜΟΝΟΥΘΥΟΥ. In light of the combination of similar-appearing letters, we might suppose that a scribe could easily have omitted these two letters accidentally. Furthermore, although a scribe might have added "God" for clarity if it was not in the original, it is unlikely that John would have failed to include the word "God" in this passage, in which God is so prominent in the discussion.

Turning to the external evidence, we find that the word "God" is omitted in some MSS and versions of the Alexandrian text-type, including very reliable ones, but it is included in other Alexandrian MSS and in the other text-types. This means that part of the text-type that is generally most reliable is opposed by another part of that same text-type and by the other text-types as well. So although the external evidence is somewhat mixed, it leans in favor of the inclusion of the word "God." The clear internal evidence reinforces this conclusion.

In Matt 7:24, on the other hand, internal evidence is not decisive but external evidence is clear. The variant is between the phrase "[he] is like a wise man" and "I will compare him to a wise man." There is little difference in meaning, and internal evidence does not give much help either way. It is possible that a copyist might have penned "I will compare him" while remembering the parallel passage in Luke 6:47, which says, "I will show you what he is like," but this seems uncertain.

The external evidence is more decisive. "He is like" is supported by the Alexandrian and most of the Western text-types, along with some of the Caesarean MSS, whereas "I will compare him" is supported primarily by the Byzantine text-type. "He is like" is thus clearly favored by external evidence, having the support of multiple text-types, including the one considered most reliable.

Finally, regarding a variant in Matt 15:38 internal and external evidence seem contradictory. Some MSS read, "besides women and children," while others have, "besides children and women." Internal evidence supports the second reading as the more difficult reading, since "children and women" is the more abnormal order. Furthermore, "women and children" occurs a bit earlier in the text (Matt 14:2), and the copyist may have conformed this passage to the earlier one. Finally, while a scribe could easily have changed "children and women" to the more normal "women and children," it seems unlikely that a scribe would have changed the normal order to the more unusual. So internal evidence favors "children and women" as the original reading on a number of grounds.

However, when it comes to the external evidence, at least part of each of the four text-types supports the reading "women and children" while the support for "children and women" is weaker. In this passage, then, internal evidence favors one reading while external evidence favors the other reading.

Let us remind ourselves again, however, that most variants entail only small differences or no differences in meaning, as is the case here. Very few variants involve readings that are doctrinally erroneous except for occasional scribal blunders that can easily be recognized.

Characteristics of the Text-Types

We have noted that assessing external evidence is an important part of deciding which is the correct reading among textual variants. In making use of this external evidence, it will be additionally helpful if we know some of the characteristics of each text-type—specifically, what kinds of readings each text-type tends to include, and also what kind of errors it tends to make and what kind of wrong readings it tends to accept. Knowing the kinds of errors a text-type is prone to include will help us to be suspicious in cases in which it appears to have a reading of that kind.

Let us consider first the Alexandrian text-type. As we have noted, it is generally the most reliable of the text-types; however, neither it nor any other text-type is always correct.

When the Alexandrian has a wrong reading, it is often a "sophisticated" change (i.e., an intentional change) rather than a careless mistake. For example, in Romans 5:1 the Alexandrian text supports the reading "let us be having peace," while the other texts support "we have peace." The difference between these two readings is merely the difference between a long o and a short o in the Greek verb "have." The correct reading is probably "we have peace." An Alexandrian scribe might have thought that "being justified by faith" implied that we do have peace with God and that Paul would not have in effect repeated himself by saying, "we have peace," but rather would have said, "let us be having peace"—that is, "let us continue to enjoy the peace we have received"—and the scribe might then have changed his MS accordingly. Other considerations in the verse substantiate the contention that "we have peace" is the original reading.

Another example of this sort of thing occurs in the story of the Prodigal Son in Luke 15:21, which we have already looked at. A large number of the Alexandrian MSS mistakenly add, "Make me like one of your hired men," probably on the assumption that the son did in fact say to his father all that he said he would in verse 19.

On the other hand, the Alexandrian text includes readings that are abrupt or terse but that prove to be correct, as well as readings that at first sight seem more difficult to understand than the alternative readings but that on further study make good sense. One example is the phrase "in order that everyone who believes may in him have eternal life" in John 3:15 instead of "that everyone who believes in him may have eternal life" (which is the text of the following verse). Another example is the reference to Jesus as "unique God" instead of "unique Son" in John 1:18.

The Western text frequently has a reading that is different from but similar to alternative readings; for example, "praising God" instead of "blessing God" in Luke 24:53 and "a hundred times as much" instead of "many times as much" in Luke 18:30. In addition, in Acts the Western reading is often a rewording of alternative readings. For example, in Acts 3:11 most MSS read, "While the beggar held on to Peter and John, all the people were astonished and came running to them in the place called Solomon's Colonnade," but the Western text reads, "And as Peter and John were going out, he [the beggar] went out together with them holding on to them; and they, astonished, stood in the colonnade."

The most puzzling type of Western reading involves omissions of a sentence or part of a sentence, especially in Acts and the final chapters of Luke. (Some scholars say that in these passages the Western text is the original and the other text-types have made additions, but most scholars consider this to be unlikely.) For example, the Western text omits the angel's words "He is not here; he has risen" in Luke 24:6, although it includes these words in Matt 28:6. The Western text also omits the phrase "blood and fire and billows of smoke" in Acts 2:19.

Characteristics of the Byzantine text include readings that provide smoother transitions, are easier to understand, or are theologically stronger than the alternatives. For example, the Byzantine text of Mark 7:5 reads, "unwashed" hands, while the alternative reading is a word that can mean either "unwashed" or "ceremonially unclean." The Byzantine text of Mark 1:2, introducing quotes of both Malachi and Isaiah, reads, "It is written in the prophets," while other MSS read, "It is written in Isaiah the prophet." The Byzantine also contains many more readings than other text-types in which one gospel passage is harmonized to agree with the parallel in another gospel.

As previously mentioned, there is some dispute among scholars as to whether the small group of Caesarean MSS constitutes a valid text-type in itself, although these texts do constitute important witnesses. For one thing, Caesarean readings are distinctive only in the Gospels. Furthermore, the Caesarean MSS do not seem to have strong unique characteristics but agree sometimes with the Alexandrian and sometimes with the Western text-types. Caesarean MSS, however, do not display the long paraphrases and omissions that characterize the Western text.

Some Witnesses to the Text-Types

The most important witnesses to the Alexandrian text-type include the papyrus codex $\mathfrak{P}^{66}$ (which was written about A.D. 150 and is one of the two oldest known New Testament MSS), $\mathfrak{P}^{75}$, Codex Aleph (ℵ, Sinaiticus), Codex B (Vaticanus), and Codex 33, as well as the Bohairic version of Egypt and the quotations of Cyril of Alexandria.

The Western text-type is contained in Codex D (05, Bezae) of the Gospels and Acts, Codex D (06, Claromontanus) of the Pauline Epistles), and the Old Latin version.

The Byzantine text-type is supported by most of the uncial MSS of the fifth century and later, by most of the minuscule MSS, and by most of the versions and church fathers of the fifth and later centuries.

Important Caesarean MSS include Codex Theta (Θ, known as the Koridethi Gospels, an uncial MS), Codex W (Cod. Washingtoniensis) of Mark from chapter 5 on, and two subgroups of minuscule MSS closely related to Cod. 1 and Cod. 13, respectively—Family 1 and Family 13. The gospel portions of the Georgian, Armenian, and Palestinian Syriac versions and the quotations of Cyril of Jerusalem also follow the Caesarean pattern.

Did Scribes Intentionally Corrupt the New Testament Text?

To admit, as we have, that scribes at times made intentional changes in the MSS they were copying may raise fears in the minds of some people that scribes may have deliberately falsified or watered down the text of the New Testament in some passages. We need have no such fears. The scribes who copied the New Testament MSS, especially in the earliest period when most of the variants developed, were doing so because they wanted to make the message available to more readers, not to change it. In later centuries, scribes were often monks who were copying the MSS as part of their religious duties, often without really under-standing the Greek they were copying. These later scribes were hardly in a position to introduce subtle heresies into their MSS. I have personally examined some seven or eight thousand New Testament variants with a good deal of care, and I would be hard pressed to make even a brief list of variants that give evidence that a scribe was attempting to weaken or falsify the message.

There were men in the early church who did, in fact, at-tempt to distort the New Testament text. One of these was the second-century teacher Marcion, who totally rejected the Old Testament and made numerous changes in the epistles to suit his own views. Marcion and others like him were not scribes, however; they were teachers. They did not advance their views by copying MSS incorrectly, even though they may have made changes in their own New Testaments. They depended instead upon teaching and publicizing their doctrines. Scribes, on the other hand, were not engaged in studying the text but simply in copying it.

In recent years it has become increasingly popular for some scholars to exaggerate the extent to which early copy-ists of the New Testament MSS intentionally altered the bibli-cal text to fit their own theological prejudices. Some of these scholars argue that these intentional or theological textual corruptions have significantly distorted the message given by the original biblical authors.[1] Such critics bolster their ar-gument by citing the total number of variations between all known New Testament MSS. Estimates reach as high as four hundred thousand variants, which is more than the number of words in the entire New Testament.

While it may be possible to argue that on rare occa-sions intentional modifications were made to New Testa-ment MSS, there are several reasons to conclude that these claims of purposeful textual corruption have been grossly overblown. Furthermore, because of the large number of New Testament MSS in existence today, textual scholars are nearly universally convinced that such intentional changes, to whatever extent they did occur, have neither seriously distorted the message of the original writers nor hampered our ability to discover the original readings in the vast majority of cases.

Since the early days of the study of the New Testament text, scholars at the forefront of the field have concluded that despite the large number of minor variations between the New Testament MSS, none of these calls into question any of the central tenets of the Christian faith. Drawing upon years of intensive study of the New Testament texts at his disposal, eighteenth-century text critic J. A. Bengel came to the firm conclusion that the variations between the MSS did not shake any article of evangelical doctrine.[2]

The nineteenth-century textual critics Westcott and Hort, whose critical edition of the New Testament is still considered one of the groundbreaking achievements in the history of New Testament textual criticism, concluded that the text of the New Testament is absolutely without rival among ancient writings "in the variety and fullness of the evidence on which it rests."[3] Despite the large number of New Testament texts at their disposal, Westcott and Hort were convinced that the various MSS share "a fundamentally single and identical text."[4] Even where the texts differ, they believed that the vast majority of these discrepancies could be resolved through the careful application of the well-established tenets of textual criticism. The small residue of variants that remain in question consist, for the most part, of minor differences in spelling, word order, or the insertion or deletion of the definite article. These minor variations amount, in Westcott and Hort's estimation, to no more than "a thousandth part of the whole New Testament."[5]

Though recent studies have focused on the large number of variants and the intentional character of a few of the most egregious variations, contemporary research has produced no new evidence that would necessitate a serious reevaluation of the conclusions of the earlier generations of textual critics who were convinced that the New Testament autographs have not undergone serious alteration or distortion during the process of copying. An examination of a few of the most significant variants cited by contemporary critics to support allegations of extensive and intentional corruption will suffice to demonstrate the weakness of such claims.

Three of the most extensive New Testament variants involve passages whose authenticity has long been questioned by biblical scholars. The first of these concerns the last twelve verses of the Gospel of Mark (16:9–20). Although the authenticity of this "longer ending" of Mark's gospel has long been disputed, most contemporary English translations retain the passage in some form, usually with some indication that the verses are missing from some important ancient MSS. (There is a more detailed discussion of the arguments for and against the authenticity of this passage in chapter 8.)

Although there are better ways to account for the inclusion or omission of these verses from the earliest MSS than to argue for their intentional fabrication or suppression on theological grounds, they do contain controversial material that raises questions about the motivation behind either their inclusion in or their excision from the text. Besides a small amount of historical information that roughly parallels what is found in the other gospels, these verses contain Jesus' prediction that certain "signs" would follow those who believe in him. Among them are the driving out of demons, speaking in new tongues, handling deadly snakes and ingesting poison without harm, and healing (Mark 16:17–18).

Of course, one has only to read the New Testament more broadly, and particularly the book of Acts, to realize that many miraculous signs were attributed to the early disciples, including healings (Acts 3:1–8; 5:12–16; 9:32–41; 14:9–10), speaking in new tongues (2:1–4; 10:46; 19:6), and even a case of imperviousness to snake venom (28:3–5). Similarly, Paul addressed a number of unusual phenomena that were occurring within the first-century congregation at Corinth (1 Cor 12:9–11). The fact that the occurrence of such unusual signs is recorded in undisputed passages in the broader context of the New Testament makes the necessity of attempting to alter a significant portion of one of the gospels (either to include or to remove references to such signs) highly unlikely.

A second important variant used to support the thesis of the intentional distortion of the New Testament text concerns the account of the woman brought to Jesus after being caught in the act of adultery (John 7:53–8:11). This is another passage that New Testament scholars have long disputed. (Again, the evidence for its authenticity is discussed in greater detail in chapter 8.) The controversial element here seems to be that Jesus deals with a notorious sinner in a sympathetic, non-condemning way that may encourage a lax attitude with regard to sexual immorality. It is certainly true that the passage raises important moral questions and that it has potentially controversial implications. However, this single incident does not impact any central tenet of Christian teaching either by its inclusion or deletion. There are, in fact, other undisputed New Testament passages in which Jesus deals with notorious sinners in sympathetic ways, such as when he allowed a woman of ill repute to anoint and wash his feet (Luke 7:36–50).

A third passage that has been used to support the notion that the New Testament text has undergone intentional distortion is found in 1 John 5:7–8, the so-called "Johannine Comma." The KJV, following a few late MSS of the Latin Vulgate, reads:

> 7For there are three that bear record *in heaven, the Father, the Word, and the Holy Ghost: and these three are one.* 8*And there are three that bear witness in earth,* the Spirit, and the water, and the blood: and these three agree in one.

The Greek words underlying the italicized wording above are not included in the oldest New Testament MSS, and are thus omitted in modern critical editions of the Greek New Testament and in all early contemporary translations. (The historical debate surrounding this verse has already been discussed in chapter 5.) In place of the longer reading, the NIV reads:

> 7For there are three that testify: 8the Spirit, the water and the blood; and the three are in agreement.

At first glance it might seem that if ever there were a textual variant that called into question a central tenet of Christian theology, this would be it. Were it authentic, the longer statement would provide a strong piece of biblical support for the doctrine of the Trinity. It is certainly conceivable that someone opposed to the doctrine of the Trinity would want to excise these words from the text. By the same token, it could be argued that the discussion of "three that testify" in the shorter reading could well have triggered an overzealous Trinitarian scribe to add the words of the longer reading.

The ease with which we can imagine an intentional modification of the text in this passage, however, should be counterbalanced by the realization that the doctrine of the Trinity does not rest on the reference to the heavenly witnesses in 1 John 5:7–8. Nor does the absence of these verses put the doctrine in jeopardy, since Trinitarians have long held that the teaching rests firmly on a number of other biblical passages and lines of evidence. Indeed, assuming that the longer reading represents the insertion of inauthentic material into the text, the scribe who, for whatever reason, first inserted these words regarding the "three that bear record in heaven" no doubt did so because he was already convinced of the unity of the three divine persons on other grounds.

Indeed, the New Testament contains a number of passages in which the three persons of the Trinity are mentioned together in divine references. Consider the following examples of New Testament contexts where the three persons are mentioned in close proximity:

I urge you, brothers, by our *Lord Jesus Christ* and by the love of *the Spirit*, to join me in my struggle by praying to *God* for me (Rom 15:30, emphasis added);

May the grace of *the Lord Jesus Christ*, and the love of *God*, and the fellowship of *the Holy Spirit* be with you all (2 Cor 13:14, emphasis added);

. . . chosen according to the foreknowledge of *God the Father*, through the sanctifying work of *the Spirit*, for obedience to *Jesus Christ* and sprinkling by his blood (1 Pet 1:2, emphasis added).

But you, dear friends, build yourselves up in your most holy faith and pray in *the Holy Spirit*. Keep yourselves in *God's* love as you wait for the mercy of our *Lord Jesus Christ* to bring you to eternal life (Jude 20–21, emphasis added).

More specifically, the unity of the three divine persons can be supported by other New Testament passages, such as the following:

I and the Father are one (John 10:30);

Now *the Lord is the Spirit,* and where the Spirit of the Lord is, there is freedom (2 Cor 3:17, emphasis added);

. . . yet for us there is but *one God, the Father,* from whom all things came and for whom we live; and there is but *one Lord, Jesus Christ,* through whom all things came and through whom we live (1 Cor 8:6, emphasis added).

Finally, Jesus' statement in John 15:26 bears enough similarity to the longer reading in 1 John that it may have provided, at least in part, the basis for the disputed Vulgate tradition regarding the three heavenly witnesses: "When the Counselor comes, whom I will send to you from *the Father, the Spirit of truth* who goes out from the Father, he will testify about *me*" (emphasis added).

Other passages could be adduced to support the contention that the doctrine of the Trinity rests upon a broad, undisputed New Testament tradition. These examples will serve to illustrate that such a central Christian teaching does not stand or fall based upon a single disputed text. While a distinctly theological motivation for the insertion of the Johannine Comma cannot be ruled out, theologians convinced of the text's inauthenticity have long supported the doctrine of the Trinity from other passages that are indisputably genuine. Furthermore, those making the charge of intentional theological tampering with the New Testament text bear the burden of explaining why there are no other significant examples of attempts either to support or undermine Trinitarian theology by extensively modifying the New Testament text.

What conclusion can we draw as a result of our brief examination of these three passages that contain variants often cited as examples of intentional corruption of the New Testament text? These variations offer scant evidence of purposeful theological tampering with the New Testament text. On the contrary, these examples illustrate the ineffectiveness of any such attempts to reshape or redirect the church's theological convictions by means of textual modification. Since the key doctrinal formulations adopted by the church throughout its history have rested not on a single passage here or there, but on several lines of biblical evidence, the intentional or unintentional modification of one or two verses has posed no significant threat to the church's foundational doctrinal affirmations. Indeed, the fact that such attempts have been so rare supports the contention that attempts at intentional tweaking of the New Testament text has played no significant role in the history of the text.

CHAPTER EIGHT

Looking at Some
New Testament Variants

Let us now look at some New Testament variants, using both internal and external evidence. To keep matters simple, we will generally refer to text-types rather than to individual MSS in considering external evidence.

In dealing with the variants in the following pages, it will not be practical to present a detailed evaluation of the external evidence in making our decisions, since this evidence is often complicated and not easily presented in the brief form used here. Instead, we will simply try to discern the conclusion toward which the external evidence points. Our guidelines concerning this external evidence will be in accord with what we noted earlier about the reliability of the text-types: no text-type is infallible, but in general the Alexandrian text-type is considered most reliable, followed by the Western and Byzantine types. Caesarean witnesses will also be cited as corroborating evidence. In addition, support by more than one text-type is preferable to support by only one text-type, other things being equal. Moreover, a text-type should be suspect when it has a variant reading involving the type of error it frequently makes.

Variants with Little Difference in Meaning

The great majority of textual variants involve little or no difference in meaning. They are of importance primarily to the scholar who is studying details of the text, but they also help show us that most of the changes scribes made were *not* included for the purpose of changing the meaning of the text. Let us sample some variants of this type.

In Matt 12:15, speaking of the numbers of those who followed Jesus, some MSS read, "many crowds" (i.e., "great multitudes") where others simply read, "many." If simply "many" is original, a scribe might have added "crowds," since "many crowds" is a common expression in the Gospels; but if "many crowds" is original, there would seem to be no good reason for a scribe to omit "crowds." In this instance, then, the internal evidence favors "many" as the original reading. When we look at the external evidence, we find that the support for "many" is good but not decisive, leaving the decision in doubt. Since internal evidence favors "many" and external evidence is doubtful, we will accept "many" as the original. The difference in meaning between the two readings is, of course, virtually nothing.

In Matt 22:30, citing Jesus' teaching about what people will be like in the afterlife, some MSS read, "they will be like angels in heaven," while others read, "they will be like angels of God in heaven." If "angels of God" was original, there is no apparent reason for a scribe to have omitted "of God." However, since the Greek word for "angels" can also have a general meaning of "messengers," a scribe could have added "of God" to make the identification more specific. Internal evidence thus favors the shorter reading, "angels."

As for external evidence, both readings have some support from all the text-types. While the support for "angels" includes a few of the leading MSS of the Alexandrian and Western text-types, the evidence for "angels of God" is much more extensive. In considering both types of evidence together, however, the reasoning behind the internal evidence seems compelling enough for us to accept its conclusion in spite of the somewhat greater external support for the longer reading. So we conclude that the original reading was simply "angels." Once again, the sense is the same for either reading.

Luke 4:17 offers a historically tantalizing variant involving the two verbs "opened" and "unrolled." Some MSS state that Jesus "unrolled the scroll" of the Prophet Isaiah to read, while others state that Jesus "opened the scroll." "Unrolled" is an appropriate word to use with reference to a scroll, which is what Jesus was reading. If "unrolled" is original, a scribe might possibly have changed it to "opened" because that word is more common (the word "unrolled" occurs nowhere else in the New Testament) or because he was thinking of a book in codex form, which would be opened rather than unrolled. On the other hand, if "opened" was original, it is possible but less likely that a scribe would have changed it to the specific word for opening a scroll, "unrolled." Indeed, a related word meaning "rolled up" occurs in verse 20. Internal evidence therefore appears to favor "unrolled" slightly. In external evidence, "unrolled" has good support from all text-types and appears to be favored, even though one of the best Alexandrian witnesses supports "opened." In conclusion, even though both internal and external evidence are mixed, the lines of evidence appear to lean toward "unrolled," and so we will accept that meaning. Once again, the difference involves only a technical detail of meaning.

In Matt 8:25 the question is whether the disciples cried, "Lord, save!" as some MSS read, or "Lord, save us!" as other MSS read. Considering internal evidence, if "us" was in the original, a scribe would hardly have omitted it, whereas if the original was the more abrupt "Lord, save!" a scribe could easily have added "us" either unthinkingly or intentionally. In external evidence, the best Alexandrian MSS read, "save," corroborated by the Caesarean witnesses. "Save us" is Western and Byzantine. Although in this case two text-types oppose the shorter reading, the Byzantine text-type may in this case be dependent on the Western. In that case the strength of the Alexandrian testimony makes "save" more likely. Thus, both lines of evidence support "Lord, save!" without the addition of "us." Again, the meaning is the same for both readings.

In 2 Thess 2:3, did Paul write, "man of sin" or "man of lawlessness"? Both words make good sense. "Lawlessness," however, is a much less common word in Paul's writings than is "sin," and a scribe is more likely to have changed an uncommon word to the more common one than vice versa. Also, Paul's use of "lawlessness" in verse 7 may presuppose its use in this verse. As for MS evidence, support for "lawlessness" is limited to the Alexandrian text-type, but includes the best and most ancient Alexandrian MSS. "Sin" has broader text-type support, but the witnesses for it are generally later. In conclusion, the internal evidence, coupled with the superior Alexandrian MS support, favors "lawlessness" as the original reading. As in the previous examples, there is no essential difference in sense between the readings.

Harmonizations

A class of variants we noted earlier consists of instances in which one passage has been changed to agree with a similar or parallel passage in another book. Most of these are found in the Synoptic Gospels—Matthew, Mark, and Luke—but a few occur elsewhere.

In Matt 1:25 there are two readings—"until she gave birth to a son" and "until she gave birth to her firstborn son." There is no reason for a scribe to have omitted "her firstborn" if it was in his text, but a scribe might have added it if it was not in his text. It seems all the more likely that the phrase "her firstborn" was added to an original that did not include it because the parallel passage in Luke 2:7 reads, "she bore her firstborn son," and a scribe could easily have borrowed the phrase either intentionally or unintentionally from that source. "A son" is supported by the most ancient and reliable witnesses of the Alexandrian text-type as well as the Caesarean texts, whereas "firstborn son" has some support from all text-types. The external evidence is therefore somewhat mixed, but the strong internal evidence leads us to accept "a son" as the original text.

The Lord's Prayer is recorded both in Matt 6:9–13 and in Luke 11:2–4. In Matthew the prayer begins, "Our Father in heaven." In some MSS of Luke the prayer has the same reading as Matthew, while others simply begin the prayer with "Father." Internal evidence strongly favors "Father " as Luke's original wording, since it is the shorter reading and since the addition is likely to have been made under the influence of the text of Matthew, which had become widely used in public and private devotions. Manuscript evidence for "who is in heaven" is fairly extensive, including MSS from all text-types. However, the support for "Father " includes the best and most ancient Alexandrian MSS. The strong support for the shorter reading by internal evidence plus the ancient external support provides strong evidence that the reading "Father " was the original text of Luke 11:2.

In our earlier discussion of harmonizations we dealt with Col 1:14. We noted that internal evidence, the evidence of probability, indicates clearly that Paul did not include the phrase "through his blood" when he wrote this verse, but that it was added by a later scribe drawing on the parallel passage in Eph 1:7. We can now look at the external evidence for this variant. None of the text-types—not even the Byzantine—supports the inclusion of "through his blood" in Colossians; it appears in only a few individual MSS and other witnesses. On the other hand, as we noted in the earlier discussion, all three text-types include "through his blood" in Ephesians, which negates the charge that it was omitted from Colossians in order to weaken the passage theologically.

Although this reading has very little textual support, it did happen to be included in the MS of Colossians that Erasmus used in making his Greek New Testament edition in 1516. In this way the phrase came into the Textus Receptus version of Colossians and was then passed on to the KJV. But internal and external evidence indicate beyond any doubt that although Paul did include the phrase in Ephesians, he did not include it in Colossians.

Some Interesting Variants

Let us now look at some variants that are interesting for one reason or another without being theologically important. One variant that I believe unnecessarily tantalizes textual scholars is found in Mark 6:22. In this passage concerning the famous dance by the daughter of Herodias that cost John the Baptist his head, there are three variants: one reading refers to the girl who performed the dance as "the daughter of Herodias herself" or "Herodias's daughter herself"; a second reading is commonly taken to mean "his daughter Herodias." In a third reading, a number of versions have simply dropped the pronoun "herself" or "his" and read, "the daughter of Herodias."

Looking at internal evidence, the first and third readings make good sense; if either of these was original, there would have been no reason for a scribe to introduce the second one. The second reading, however, is the more difficult or problematic reading, since the girl was not the daughter of Herod, and her name was not Herodias. If this second reading was original, a scribe could easily have been tempted to alter two letters of the Greek pronoun "his" to change the meaning to "herself" (the first variant) or to drop the pronoun completely (the third variant).

Turning to external evidence, we find that the second reading is supported by the best Alexandrian texts and Codex D, a prominent Western MS. The first reading also has strong support, including witnesses from all the major text-types and the Caesarean manuscripts as well. Support for the third reading is not as strong as either of the other two. When the strong internal evidence is combined with the more ambiguous external evidence, the support seems to lean somewhat in favor of the first reading—and this in spite of the difficulty the passage might have posed to the scribes who copied it. It is the reading adopted by the UBS *GNT*, albeit with their least confident ranking.

While we prefer the more difficult reading in Mark 6:22, we needn't conclude that the wording involves a historical error on the part of the gospel writer Mark. Instead of reading the Greek phrase as "his daughter Herodias," we can read it as "his daughter of Herodias," meaning "his daughter—that is, Herodias's" (i.e., "his stepdaughter, who was actually the daughter of his wife Herodias"). This construction is admittedly a bit awkward, but I believe that Mark could have written it, and I do not see how the pronoun "his" could have been introduced by a scribe if it were not original.

Luke 6:1–10 deals with the observance of the Sabbath laws. At the end of verse 4, Codex D adds this brief item: "On the same day, [Jesus] saw someone working on the Sabbath and said to him, 'Man, if you know what you are doing, you are blessed; but if you do not know, you are accursed and a transgressor of the law.'"[6] This story fits the context of the chapter, and the incident may be true, but since it is found in only one MS, we cannot even consider the possibility of its being a part of the original text.

In Eph 1:1, some MSS omit the words "in Ephesus." These words could hardly have been missing originally, even though some scholars believe they were; without them the Greek text is awkward. And they could not easily have been omitted accidentally. It can be rendered in English fairly acceptably as "to the saints who are also faithful," but this raises the serious question of why Paul would have put this emphasis on the "faithful" saints. Actually the Greek very likely would be "to the saints who are, and faithful," as a reference to the greetings in Phil 1:1 suggests. Some commentators have suggested that Paul intended that this letter be copied and sent to several churches and that he left a blank space after "are" so that the appropriate destination could be inserted into each copy. However, no other destinations or churches are named here in any known MS of this epistle (although the heretical teacher Marcion did call it the epistle to the church in Laodicea). Internal evidence, then, favors the inclusion of the phrase "in Ephesus."

As for MS evidence, some of the best Alexandrian texts plus the early papyrus 𝔓⁴⁶ support the omission, while the Western, Byzantine, and part of the Alexandrian support the inclusion of the phrase. This might seem to leave the external evidence in doubt, and indeed, the UBS *GNT* includes the words translated "in Ephesus" in brackets, indicating the editors' uncertainty about the authenticity of the words. However, as we pointed out in the preceding chapter, the Alexandrian text sometimes makes a "sophisticated" error— that is, an intentional change that has some reason and thought behind it but is nevertheless wrong. This may be such an instance: an Alexandrian scribe, knowing the tradition that this letter was sent to several churches, may have taken it upon himself to omit the designation "in Ephesus." In conclusion, then, although the MS support for the omission is fairly strong, it is the type of error that the Alexandrian text sometimes makes. Moreover, the support for the inclusion of "in Ephesus" is broader, and internal evidence strongly supports the inclusion.

In Rev 12:18 (or, in some versions, 13:1), some MSS read, "And I stood on the shore of the sea," and others read, "And he stood on the shore of the sea." The difference is only a matter of the inclusion or omission of the Greek letter *n*. "He stood" fits in with the preceding verses, which refer to the activities of the dragon. "I stood" fits in with the verb "I saw" that follows immediately in 13:1. However, a study of the structure of Revelation shows that the words "And I saw" almost always indicate the beginning of a new section. On this assumption, 12:18 should be at the end of the preceding section referring to the dragon, and "he stood" would more likely be the original. As for MS evidence, "I stood" is probably Byzantine, while "he stood" is clearly Alexandrian and enjoys the support of some of its witnesses, including $\mathfrak{P}^{47}$. Thus, both internal and external evidence indicate that the original text is "he stood on the shore of the sea."

In 1 Cor 11:29 the two readings entail the inclusion and omission of the word "unworthily" in the verse: "For anyone who eats and drinks [unworthily] without recognizing the body of the Lord eats and drinks judgment on himself." If "unworthily" was in the original text, there would be no reason for it to have been omitted intentionally, since that is clearly the sense of the verse; nor is there any basis for supposing that it would have been omitted accidentally. On the other hand, if "unworthily" was not in the original text, a scribe, thinking that "without recognizing" meant that the partaker comes under judgment *because* he does not recognize" the Lord's body, and that the verse would therefore seem to condemn everyone, could easily have added "unworthily." However, "without recognizing the body" can also mean that the partaker is condemned *"if* he does not recognize the body," which does not require the word "unworthily." From internal evidence we therefore conclude that the omission is preferred. As for MS evidence, "unworthily" is supported by the Byzantine and Western texts, while the omission is supported by the Alexandrian text-type plus the early papyrus $\mathfrak{P}^{46}$. Both internal and external evidence thus support the text without "unworthily," with "without recognizing the body" meaning "if he does not recognize the body."

At the end of the same verse, after "without recognizing the body" some MSS omit the phrase "of the Lord." This latter phrase would not easily have been omitted accidentally if it were original; and there would have been no reason for even a heretic to omit it intentionally, since "the body" is clearly the Lord's body. On the other hand, if the phrase was not original, a scribe could easily have added it in order to leave no doubt about the meaning. The MS evidence for and against the inclusion of the phrase are almost exactly the same as for the addition and omission of "unworthily." Again, both internal and external evidence agree, and we conclude that what Paul wrote here was simply "without recognizing the body."

Sometimes the scribes have really warmed to their work and have developed a great variety of readings in a particular passage. In Mark 6:33, for example, a considerable assortment of variants for "got there ahead of them" in the phrase "[they] ran on foot from all the towns and got there ahead of them" have accumulated, including the following: "came to them," "came together there," "came there," "got there ahead of them," "came together to him," "got there ahead of them and came together to him," and others. The phrase "got there ahead of them" has good internal support, since scribes may have made the changes because they felt that it was unlikely that the crowds on foot could have arrived before the boat did. External evidence also favors "got there ahead of them."

Colossians 2:2 also has an assortment of readings. The MS evidence favors "in order that they may know the mystery of God, *namely,* Christ." However, since it is possible to misunderstand the Greek text as saying, "the mystery of God *of* Christ," scribes apparently tried to clarify the text in various ways, producing such variants as "the mystery of Christ," "the mystery of God and of Christ," "the mystery of God, namely Christ," "the mystery of God who is in Christ," "the mystery of God the father in Christ Jesus," "the mystery of God the father of Christ," "the mystery of God the father of Jesus Christ," "the mystery of God the Father and of Christ," "the mystery of the God and Father of Christ," and "the mystery of the God and Father and of Christ." A careful study of these many readings can show how they developed from the simple original. It is important to note, however, that in this very theologically meaningful passage none of the variant readings show any attempt to weaken or distort the theology.

Galatians 4:7 is another passage in which scribes have developed a multitude of readings. The MS evidence supports "and if [you are] a child, then [you are] also an heir, *through God*" (NRSV). It is more natural, however, to think of our being heirs through Christ than through God, although the latter concept is reasonable (cf. 1 Cor 1:9). This apparent problem led scribes of various MSS to change "through God" to "of God," "because of God," "through Christ," "through Jesus Christ," "of God through Christ," "of God through Jesus Christ," "through God in Jesus Christ," and "of God and joint heir of Christ." Once again, however, the reading that has the strongest external support is the one that best explains the others. Notice again also that not one of these readings shows any attempt to corrupt this theologically significant passage.

Romans 4:19 has a variant of two readings that seem at first to be contradictory: Abraham "considered his own body, which was already as good as dead" (NRSV) and "did not consider his own body, which was already as good as dead." The contradiction, however, is only a matter of appearance, not substance. The first reading means that even though Abraham recognized that his body was too old, he nevertheless did not hesitate to believe God's promise that he would have a son. The second reading means that because of God's promise, Abraham did *not* consider his body too old to enable him to become a father. Both readings, then, make good sense, although "considered" requires a bit of thought to understand the argument, while "did not consider" is easier to grasp at first sight. So it is more likely that "considered" was changed to "did not consider" than vice versa. "Considered" is the Alexandrian reading; "did not consider" is Western and Byzantine. Both internal and external evidence, therefore, support "considered." Whichever reading is assumed to be original, however, it is important to note that the change was not an attempt to weaken the text or introduce a false teaching.

It is remarkable how much difference in meaning one small Greek letter can make. In Luke 2:14, for example, if the final word in the Greek text ends with an *s*, the meaning is "upon earth peace among men of good will" (literal translation). If the final word ends without an *s*, the meaning is "on earth peace, goodwill toward men" (NKJV). In the first reading it is possible that "men of good will" could refer to people who have an attitude of good will toward others, but it much more likely means "peace to men on whom his favor rests" (i.e., peace on those with whom he is pleased), as the NIV and most modern versions interpret the passage.

The question is whether Luke wrote that final Greek *s* or not. The form without the *s* is easier to interpret; indeed, its meaning is so obvious that it is very improbable that a scribe would have changed it intentionally. On the other hand, if the *s* was original, a scribe might have omitted it intentionally to make the reading easier to understand, or he might have omitted it accidentally, since the Greek *s* at the end of a line was sometimes written as a very small raised letter. Internal evidence, then, favors the reading with the *s*.

In MS evidence, the form with the *s* is supported by the best part of the Alexandrian and Western texts, while the other form is Caesarean and Byzantine, so the inclusion of the *s* is preferred on these grounds as well. Thus both internal and external evidence favor the reading "upon earth peace to men with whom God is pleased."

In 1 John 3:1, following "How great is the love the Father has lavished on us, that we should be called children of God!" some MSS add the words "And that is what we are!" Could this be a case of a heretical scribe deliberately omitting this phrase to eliminate the strong assertion that we are not only *called* children of God but truly *are* his children? If so, it is heresy perpetuated by the Byzantine text-type, the Textus Receptus, and the KJV! We can safely say that it is *not* an intentional heretical omission, however, because the MSS that omit "And that is what we are!" agree with all other MSS in reading, "Dear friends, now we are children of God," in the very next verse. On the other hand, if the author did not originally include this phrase, a well-meaning scribe could have added it to strengthen the passage, wanting to make it clear that we truly *are* God's children.

There is another possibility, however: it might have been an unintentional error. In Greek uncial letters, the phrase "and we are" closely resembles the letters immediately preceding them in this verse; it consists of the last seven letters of the following sequence: ΚΛΗΘΩΜΕΝΚΑΙΕϹΜΕΝ. A scribe's eye could easily have skipped from the first ΜΕΝ to the second, causing him to omit the last seven letters. It thus appears that "and we are" could have been either added intentionally or omitted unintentionally.

Manuscript evidence is overwhelmingly in favor of the inclusion of the phrase. The Alexandrian and Western texts include it; only the Byzantine text, which more often adds words than omits them, omits these words. Combining this strong external evidence with the internal evidence, we may confidently conclude that John originally included the phrase "and we are" and that subsequent scribes accidentally omitted it.

Another interesting variant occurs in 1 John 4:20, of which the readings are "[he] cannot love God, whom he has not seen" and "how is he able to love God, whom he has not seen?" An accidental error seems unlikely in this case even though the difference in the Greek text is a matter of only two words of two and three letters respectively. As for intentional change, a scribe might have felt that "he is not able" was too absolute and softened it to "how is he able." Another possibility is that the scribe adopted the form of the rhetorical question for greater dramatic effect. It is also possible, but less likely, that a scribe might have intentionally changed "how is he able" to the more factual "he is not able."

In MS evidence, "he is not able" has strong Alexandrian support, while "how is he able" is Byzantine and possibly Western. Considering this evidence and the probable preference of internal evidence, we conclude that the original text is "he is not able" and that a scribe weakened it to "how is he able" not from a heretical motive but from a feeling that it might not be totally impossible for a person to love God even if he did not love his brother.

In Matt 6:1 the Alexandrian and Western texts read, "Be careful not to do your 'acts of righteousness' before men," while the Caesarean and Byzantine texts read, "alms," instead of "acts of righteousness." The external evidence thus favors "acts of righteousness," which we understand as referring to various deeds of righteousness such as those Jesus goes on to mention: alms (v. 2), prayer (v. 5), and fasting (v. 16). If "alms" was original, it would hardly have been changed by a scribe to the much less obvious "acts of righteousness." It is much more likely that a scribe thought that "acts of righteousness" in verse 1 meant the same thing as "alms" in verse 2, so he changed the more general word to the more specific word for the sake of clarity. Both internal and external evidence, then, support "righteousness" as the original text here.

In Matt 6:4, after the phrase "your Father, who sees what is done in secret, will reward you," the Byzantine text adds the word "openly," but the other three text-types omit this word. External evidence thus favors the omission. As for internal evidence, there is no apparent reason for "openly" to have been omitted either accidentally or intentionally if it was original. If it was not original, however, it would have been very easy for a scribe to add it to make a more complete contrast with the word "secretly" in the preceding clause. Both lines of evidence thus favor the omission of "openly." Jesus was making the point that God will reward righteous deeds, not necessarily that the reward will be obvious to everyone. Incidentally, the same variant occurs in verse 18 with even less MS support.

Some Important Variants

Let us now look at some more significant variants, instances in which the meaning of the passage is affected to some extent by the readings.

In Mark 1:1 most MSS read, "The beginning of the gospel about Jesus Christ, the Son of God," but some MSS omit "the Son of God." Heresy! someone cries. But let's take a closer look. First, from internal evidence we see that if Mark did not include the phrase "Son of God" here, a pious scribe could easily have added it. But if the phrase was part of the original text, would a heretical scribe have omitted it? If he did so, why would this presumed heretic leave the word "Christ," which is an exalted title for Jesus, in the text? Furthermore, the very MSS that omit "Son of God" here include these very words in Mark 15:39, in which the Roman centurion, seeing Jesus die, calls him "Son of God."

It is more likely that the phrase is original and was omitted accidentally. The last three letters of the word "gospel" plus the phrase "Jesus Christ Son of God" would have been written as ιογῑγ̄χ̄γγ̄·θ̄γ̄ in an early Greek MS. The repetition of the letter γ could have caused a scribe's eye to skip over the last four letters, which form the regular Greek abbreviation for "Son of God."

Turning to external evidence, we find that only the Alexandrian Codex Aleph (א) and some of the Caesarean witnesses omit "Son of God" here, while the rest of the Alexandrian text-type, the Western and Byzantine text-types, and the other Caesarean texts include the phrase. Manuscript evidence therefore strongly supports the inclusion of the phrase. Since internal evidence indicates that the phrase was probably omitted accidentally, we conclude from both lines of evidence that "Son of God" was part of the original text of Mark 1:1.

Another significant variant is found in Acts 8:37. After the Ethiopian official asks Philip, "Why shouldn't I be baptized?" some MSS include verse 37, as follows: "And Philip said, 'If you believe with all your heart, you may.' The eunuch answered, 'I believe that Jesus Christ is the Son of God.'" Other MSS omit this dialogue and immediately after the Ethiopian's question continue with verse 38: "And he gave orders to stop the chariot. . . ."

Verse 37 could hardly have been either added or omitted accidentally. Moreover, it is highly unlikely that the verse was intentionally omitted by a heretic wanting to eliminate this confession concerning Jesus Christ, because the same MSS that omit this verse include acknowledgments of Jesus as the Son of God a few verses later, in 9:20. On the other hand, if the author of Acts did not provide the exchange recorded in this verse, it would have been tempting for a scribe to do so, since the question in verse 36 must have received a reply.

The MS support for verse 37 is very weak, consisting only of part of the Western text. The verse is not found even in the Byzantine MSS. Although the verse appears in the Textus Receptus and therefore in the KJV, it was not in the MS Erasmus used principally for Acts in his first published Greek New Testament in 1516. He found this passage as a marginal addition to another MS of Acts and added it in a later edition, thinking that it must have been original but that it had been omitted from his other MS by accident.

The Ethiopian official surely must have confessed his faith in Jesus before Philip baptized him, either before or after he raised the question of baptism. That Philip's question and the official's confession were not part of the original text here, however, is certain on the basis of both internal and external evidence. Incidentally, if someone wonders why this addition has a verse number if it was not original, he should remember that our verse numbers were not put into the text until the fourth edition of Stephanus in 1551, as we noted earlier—long after Erasmus had included the verse.

In Mark 9:29 Jesus says of the unclean spirit he had expelled from a boy, "This kind can come out only by prayer," or as other MSS read, "by prayer and fasting." The words "and fasting" could hardly have been either added or omitted accidentally. Neither is it likely that the phrase was omitted intentionally in prejudice against fasting, because the same MSS that omit "and fasting" here include a favorable reference to fasting in Mark 2:18–20. However, if Mark did not originally include this phrase, an early scribe could easily have added it to emphasize the spiritual effort involved in the exorcism. Internal evidence, then, favors the omission of "and fasting" here.

Most MSS include "and fasting," however. Only the two best Alexandrian MSS (Codd. Aleph [א] and B), one Western witness, one Caesarean witness, and one church father's quotation omit it. External evidence, then, is doubtful but may favor the inclusion of the phrase. However, if a scribe added these words in a MS, the increasing emphasis in the early church on the necessity of fasting might have attracted other scribes to the addition even if they knew that it was not found in all MSS in their day. Internal evidence, therefore, leads to the conclusion that "and fasting" was not an original part of Mark here, even though fasting is favorably mentioned elsewhere.

It is worth noting that the phrase "and fasting" is added by some MSS in 1 Cor 7:5 as well, following the words "so that you may devote yourselves to prayer." Here, however, the MS support for the addition is only Byzantine, and it is clearly not original.

In their worship, Protestants conclude the Lord's Prayer with the doxology "for yours is the kingdom and the power and the glory forever. Amen." This version of the doxology appears in Matt 6:13 in the Byzantine text and some Alexandrian and Caesarean witnesses, while the Western text, part of the Alexandrian, and some Caesarean MSS omit it. Manuscript evidence therefore favors the omission, although not strongly.

The doxology is omitted by all witnesses from the Lord's Prayer recorded in Luke 11:2–4. It is not likely that the doxology would have been omitted either accidentally or intentionally from Matthew if it had been original. However, since without it the prayer seems to end a bit abruptly, when it came to be used in worship services, a doxology such as this could easily have been added. From this use it could have been added to the MSS by scribes who thought that its use in worship indicated that it must have been as much a part of the original text as the prayer itself. The conclusion, then, strongly from internal evidence and to a lesser degree from external evidence, is that the doxology was not part of the original text of Matthew. Of course, it is still perfectly proper to use the doxology when reciting the prayer in worship or devotions. (For a similar doxology, see 1 Chr 29:11.) It should be remembered that when Jesus gave this prayer to his disciples, he was not giving them a liturgical form to repeat but rather was teaching them how simply and directly they could talk to their heavenly Father.

In 1 Cor 6:20 the question is whether Paul simply says, "therefore honor God with your body," or whether he adds, "and with your spirit, which are God's." The added words are a perfectly proper exhortation, but if they were original, there is no reasonable way to account for their having been omitted in so many good MSS. On the other hand, if they were not original, a devout scribe could have added them, possibly in an effort to guard against the idea that we should glorify God only with our physical bodies. We should, of course, glorify God with our spirits as well, but in this passage (1 Cor 6:12–20) the apostle is speaking specifically of the physical body, and the reference to the human spirit here is not in harmony with the context.

The omission of the reference to the spirit is strongly supported by the Alexandrian and Western text-types, while the addition is supported by the Byzantine. Both internal and external evidence, therefore, make it clear that Paul's words here are simply "therefore honor God with your body" as an emphatic summary of his discussion of the sanctity of our bodies.

Three Longer Variants

There is a textual variant in John 5:3–4 that we should examine. Following the reference to the sick people at the Pool of Bethesda in verse 3, some MSS add that they "waited for the moving of the waters. ⁴From time to time an angel of the Lord would come down and stir up the waters. The first one into the pool after each such disturbance would be cured of whatever disease he had." Other MSS omit this final part of verse 3 and all of verse 4.

That these words were original and were omitted accidentally is very unlikely, since none of the elements that commonly lead to accidental omission are present. Furthermore, an ancient scribe would have had no reason to omit this reference intentionally, since it gives relevant information. Nor would the reference to an angel's activity have been a problem for a scribe; the MSS that omit this passage freely include references to angels in other parts of the Gospels. On the other hand, if John did not originally include this explanation of the popular belief in the curative power of the pool, it would have been a very natural thing for an early copyist who knew of the tradition to add it. Indeed, a scribe might have put these words in the margin of his MS not intending to add them to the text of the gospel but simply giving a note to explain what happened at the pool. A later scribe, seeing the note in the margin of the MS as he was copying from it, might then have taken it to be a part of the gospel text that had been accidentally omitted and later added in the margin (which was done at times) and on that basis have incorporated it into his MS. The addition would then have been included in all further copies made from this MS.

Additional evidence against the likelihood that this passage was in the original MS is the fact that six or seven words or phrases in it are not used anywhere else in John's gospel; indeed, three of the words are found nowhere else in the New Testament.

As for MS evidence, the passage is omitted in the best part of the Alexandrian text, including two of the oldest papyrus MSS ($\mathfrak{P}^{66}$ and $\mathfrak{P}^{75}$), as well as part of the Western text. It is included by the Byzantine text and the Caesarean MSS and by some witnesses of the other two text-types. Many MSS that include the passage have notations indicating that it was not considered to be a part of the original text. Both the internal and the strong external evidence make it clear that this explanatory note was not part of John's text but was added later.

There are two significant passages in the New Testament in which a textual variant involves several verses. One of these is John 7:53–8:11, the story of the woman taken in adultery. The question here is not whether the story is true—as John 20:30 reminds us, Jesus did many things that are not recorded in the Gospels—but simply whether John included this story when he wrote his gospel.

Let us look at the external evidence first. We would not question the passage if it were present in all of the MSS, but it is omitted by the Alexandrian text—including Codices Aleph ($\aleph$) and B and two of the oldest papyri ($\mathfrak{P}^{66}$ and $\mathfrak{P}^{75}$)—as well as by the Western text, some of the Caesarean witnesses, and by a variety of versions and church fathers. Other MSS include the passage here but with notations indicating doubt that it is genuine. Still other MSS place the story after Luke 21:38, after John 7:36, at the very end of Luke, or at the very end of John. Furthermore, the story is not commented on by any Greek church father until the twelfth century, and the first Greek father who does so states that accurate copies of the gospel do not contain the passage. In view of the vast extent of ancient commentaries on the New Testament, it would be incredible that they would not have dealt with a story such as this if the church fathers had considered it a genuine part of John's gospel.

Among witnesses that include this passage at this point with no indication of doubt concerning it are part of the

Western text, the Byzantine text, and some other MSS and Latin church fathers that are not classified under the recognized text-types. The MS evidence, then, is decisively against considering this passage as an original part of John's gospel.

Turning to internal evidence, the passage is obviously too long to have been omitted accidentally from more than one or two MSS. But could it have been omitted intentionally by scribes who felt that the story dealt too leniently with a sin as serious as adultery? This seems unlikely, inasmuch as there is no indication that any scribes attempted to delete either the story in Luke 7:36–50 of the gentle treatment that Jesus gave to the "sinful woman" who anointed his feet or the statement in Luke 23:43 of Jesus' promise of forgiveness to the repentant thief on the cross. Furthermore, if a scribe had wished to delete this story, there would have been no necessity for him to eliminate 7:53–8:2, which would have joined well with 8:12.

It is especially significant to observe that this passage contains many Greek words and forms of words that are not in harmony with the style or vocabulary of the rest of the gospel. Indeed, one scholar pointed out a number of years ago that the passage more closely resembles the vocabulary and style of Luke than of John. In the final analysis, then, although this story may very well be true, since it is not inconsistent with other gospel accounts about Jesus, it is nevertheless clear that it cannot be called a part of the inspired gospel record.

The second of these major textual problems involves the ending of Mark. The Alexandrian Codices Sinaiticus and Vaticanus (Aleph [א] and B) both omit Mark 16:9–20, as does the second-century church father Cyril of Alexandria and a few other witnesses. In addition, the Ammonian Sections (a system of section divisions for each of the gospels developed in the early fourth century that is something like our verse divisions but generally longer) stop at Mark 16:8. Two third-century church fathers who quote Scripture very extensively make no reference to these closing verses in their writings. Among the MSS that do contain these verses, some have notations indicating that there is doubt that they are part of the original text, while others insert the following brief passage before verse 9 to smooth the otherwise rough transition between verses 8 and 9: "Then they briefly reported all this to Peter and his companions. Afterward Jesus himself sent them out from east to west with the sacred and unfailing message of salvation that gives eternal life. Amen" (NLT). In addition, one fifth-century MS also includes a ninety-word addition following verse 14.

Although the great majority of the MSS and versions do contain verses 9–20, the evidence for the omission of these verses is too strong to be passed over. Let us consider the factors involved.

If the Greek text of 16:9–20 harmonized with the rest of the gospel, we would be inclined to suppose that these verses had been accidentally omitted from the witnesses mentioned above. For one thing, if the verses are omitted, the gospel is left with no record of the appearances of Jesus after his resurrection. Indeed, the gospel without these verses ends on a note of pessimism and frustration: "Trembling and bewildered, the women went out and fled from the tomb. They said nothing to anyone, because they were afraid." More than this, the final word in the Greek text is the conjunction "for" ("because" in the NIV). The Greek "for" cannot stand first in a clause, so it follows the Greek verb "they were afraid" here. However, ending a sentence with "for," while not impossible, would be somewhat unusual. The reader would normally expect more words to follow.

The problem, however, is not so simple. The words and forms in these verses are so different from the rest of the gospel that a student who had read Mark in Greek up to this point but had not read any of the rest of the New Testament in Greek would find himself in unfamiliar material in these last verses. Furthermore, as we have noted, the connection between verses 8 and 9 is exceedingly harsh. The subject changes from "the women" in verse 8 to "Jesus" in verse 9, and yet Jesus is not named. In verse 9 the writer tells us who Mary Magdalene is, although she has already been named in verse 1. There is another small but significant point. In the seven other instances in the New Testament in which the phrase "the first day of the week" occurs, including one instance in Mark 16:2, the Greek form is literally "day one" rather than "the first day." Yet in Mark 16:9 the form is "the first day"—which sounds better in English but is not the characteristic New Testament form.

If, then, verses 9–20 are not an original part of the gospel, what do we make of the situation? One possibility is that the original ending of Mark was lost at a very early date and that a scribe wrote verses 9–20 in an attempt to supply a suitable ending for the gospel. Another is that despite the abruptness of the language, the original gospel ended at 16:8.

How might the final part of the gospel have been lost? Early in this book we noted that the original MSS—the autographs—of the gospels were written on papyrus, likely in scroll form. When someone finished reading a scroll, the outer part of the scroll would be the end of the book if the reader did not bother to reroll it. It is possible that the autograph of Mark, or a very early copy, could have been left without being rerolled, in which case the last one or two spirals of the scroll could have been accidentally torn off. On the other hand, we also noted that at a very early date MSS of the New Testament were also produced in codex form, like our present books; it is possible that even the original or at least one of the earliest copies was produced in this form. If this were the case, it would have been even easier for the final quire or the final one or two sheets to have been torn off accidentally, leaving the gospel with the abrupt ending at 16:8.

In summary, both external and internal evidence strongly indicates that verses 9–20 as we know them were not part of the gospel of Mark as originally written. The original ending of Mark may have been lost very soon after it was written. It is also possible that the original Gospel of Mark simply ended somewhat abruptly at 16:8.

CHAPTER NINE

The New Testament Text and Modern Translations

Translations and Textual History

While the field of textual criticism is of great interest to those who interact directly with the Greek text, some may wonder what value it offers to the non-specialist whose reading of the Bible is limited to one or the other English translation. How much can the English reader benefit from an understanding of textual criticism? This question can be addressed either from the broad perspective of which Bible translations use which types of text or from the narrow perspective of how to deal with the discrete variations one encounters when reading particular passages.

Concerning the broader question, the history of Bible translation provides a good opportunity to assess the importance of the field of textual criticism to biblical studies as a whole. Understandably, discussions of the multitude of translations available today continue to stir controversy. Perhaps the most vigorous contemporary debate concerns on the one hand those who call for a return to the KJV, based as it is on the Byzantine text-type represented in the great majority of Greek MSS, and on the other hand those who advocate the use of one or another of the contemporary Bible translations that rest upon a modern critical text that often departs from the Byzantine tradition.

In assessing where a particular translation stands in relation to the history of the New Testament text, it is important to bear in mind the broad contours of that history as it relates to the various text-types that prevailed in different regions of the ancient world. We laid out that history in greater detail in chapter 4, so a brief review of it will be sufficient here. For most of its history, the Eastern church used and made copies of MSS that were, by and large, of the *Byzantine* text-type. Most contemporary textual scholars, following earlier textual critics such as Tischendorf and Westcott/Hort, believe that these Byzantine copies were derived from an original that was produced by combining two earlier text-types, the Alexandrian and the Western. A small number of contemporary scholars, however, continue to defend the Byzantine type as the type that is closest to the autographs. The Western church, throughout the medieval period, relied largely on the Latin Vulgate translation, which in turn was made from MSS largely of the *Western* text-type. Westcott and Hort argued that the Western type, although in some cases closer to the autographs than the Byzantine, nevertheless represented an edited text that was smoothed out in many places by adding explanatory words or by modifying the text in other minor ways. The views of Westcott and Hort continue to guide the thinking of most contemporary textual scholars.

In the eyes of Westcott and Hort and most textual critics since their time, the text-type closest to the New Testament autographs is the *Alexandrian* text-type, although recent textual scholars do not share the level of confidence in it that Westcott and Hort initially held. While they accept the broad outlines of textual history laid out by Westcott and Hort, current scholars tend to look at the Alexandrian text with more of a critical eye with respect to differences within its own textual tradition and in the light of contexts in which prominent Alexandrian MSS may not seem to preserve the most accurate readings. In places where the Alexandrian tradition seems doubtful, contemporary textual scholars use an eclectic approach dependent on both external (MS) evidence and internal evidence—evidence found within the text itself. On occasion, that internal evidence seems to point to the authenticity of a distinctly Western or even a distinctively Byzantine reading. This eclectic approach is best represented today in the work of the Editorial Committee of the United Bible Societies responsible for the publication of the UBS4 *GNT* and its companion *Textual Commentary*.

If this eclectically modified Alexandrian text forms the basis for the editions of the printed Greek New Testament most often preferred among contemporary scholars, it is no surprise that virtually all of the major modern English versions are based on a similar text. Among these are the American and New American Standard, the Revised and New Revised Standard, the Living and New Living, the New International and Today's New International, the English Standard Version, and the NET Bible. This doesn't imply that each of these translations follows the UBS Greek text unswervingly, since the various translation committees have made their own judgments regarding particular variants. However, these translations' departures from the NA/UBS text are relatively rare.

Only a small number of current English versions exclusively represent the Western and Byzantine textual traditions. The Douay-Rheims Version, popular among Roman Catholics, predated the KJV by just two years. It was originally a translation of Jerome's Latin Vulgate, a clear representative of the Western textual tradition. The original translators were in fact convinced that the Vulgate preserved a less corrupted form of the text than the (predominantly Byzantine) extant Hebrew and Greek MSS of the time. However, in 1752 Bishop Challoner published a thorough revision of Douay-Rheims based not only on a corrected version of the Vulgate but on Hebrew and Greek texts as well, thus moving the version in a decidedly more Byzantine/KJV direction. Most editions of the Douay-Rheims Version today are based on this less distinctively Western Challoner revision. Nearly all of the English translations that exclusively reflect the Byzantine text-type are revisions of the 1611 KJV. The best known of these is the New King James Version (NKJV), published in 1982.

Contemporary Translations and Textual Variants

While the history of the New Testament text advanced by modern textual scholars has dramatically influenced the field of Bible translation, the various contemporary English versions differ somewhat in the way they reflect variations in the original text. Readers desiring to be aware of significant contexts in which the New Testament MSS differ should be careful to consult a translation that includes information about variant readings and should pay close attention to the kinds of information presented and the manner in which variants are characterized.

The following survey of some of the leading contemporary translations illustrates how different English versions handle New Testament variants. To make the survey more concrete, a sample text, the conclusion of the Lord's Prayer in Matt 6:13, has been used. We noted earlier (chapter 8) that MSS in the Byzantine textual tradition contain a concluding doxology for the Lord's Prayer: "For yours is the kingdom and the power and the glory forever. Amen." Manuscripts of the Western text-type, however, lack the concluding doxology, while the Alexandrian tradition is divided, with the earlier MSS lacking the wording and some of the later ones including it.

New International Version (NIV)

According to the preface to the New International Version (International Bible Society, 1984), the Greek text used for the translation of the New Testament was "an eclectic one," drawing from an abundance of available MS witnesses. At the same time, the preface indicates that "the best current printed texts of the Greek New Testament were used." Where variants occur within the MS evidence, judgments were made "according to accepted principles of New Testament textual criticism." Throughout the text of the translation, "footnotes call attention to places where there was uncertainty about what the original text was." The footnote at Matt 6:13 informs the reader that "some late manuscripts" contain the wording of the doxology. By referring to the MS support for the doxology as "late," the NIV note contains the implicit judgment that the inclusion of the doxology is based on an inferior textual tradition.

New Revised Standard Version (NRSV)

The New Revised Standard Version (Nelson, 1989), in its preface "To the Reader," states explicitly that the text used for the translation of the New Testament is based on the third edition of the UBS *GNT.*[7] The preface goes on to explain that "in very rare instances" the translators departed from the UBS text where a particular variant reading seemed superior. As in the UBS, brackets are sometimes used to indicate words that have been "generally regarded to be later additions to the text" but have been retained because of their antiquity or importance within the textual tradition. Yet despite the translators' general adherence to the UBS, they include marginal notes throughout the text that point to significant textual variants from the UBS base. The marginal note for Matt 6:13 illustrates the version's standard procedure in dealing with variants, stating in the most general terms that "Other ancient authorities add, in some form," the words of the doxology.

New Living Translation (NLT)

The preface of the New Living Translation (Tyndale House, 2004) states that textual footnotes are included where passages vary from a form of the text that is "very familiar (usually through the KJV)." In most cases this means that a variant will be highlighted when the NLT departs from the KJV/Byzantine textual tradition. Textual footnotes are also used when the text follows a variant that differs from "the Hebrew and Greek editions normally followed," which likely indicates when the translators have chosen to deviate from the UBS text. In Matt 6:13, the NLT footnote makes the general comment that "Some manuscripts add" the doxology, leaving the reader uninformed as to whether the variant in this context signals a departure from the UBS text or (as in this case) the Byzantine text.

New English Translation (NET)

While the NET Bible (Biblical Studies Press, 1996), like most other contemporary English translations, is based on a form of the Greek text similar to UBS/NA27, the introduction to the first edition states that "an eclectic text was followed, differing in several hundred places from the standard critical text as represented by the Nestle-Aland 27th edition."[8] Significant variant readings are indicated in text-critical notes, indicated by the [tc] symbol, which often include extended discussions of the evidence favoring particular readings and even the citation of principal ancient MSS, versions, and church fathers. In each passage where the NET Bible departs from the NA27 text, the difference is specially marked in a text-critical note. An extensive text-critical note is included at Matt 6:13 supporting the omission of the doxology and explaining the probable origins of the added wording. In addition, specific manuscripts, versions, and quotations from early church fathers are cited on both sides. See the discussion below under "Other Textual Tools" for a more detailed discussion of the NET Bible's handing of this variant.

English Standard Version (ESV)

In its preface, the English Standard Version (Crossway, 2001) explicitly states that the translation is based on the fourth edition of the UBS *GNT* and the twenty-seventh edition of the *NTG*.[9] The translators make it clear, however, that in "a few difficult cases" they have departed from the UBS/NA text. In these cases the textual footnotes, said to be "an integral part of the ESV translation," inform the reader about "textual variations and difficulties" and how these have been resolved. The footnotes are also said to point out "significant alternative readings" or to clear up "a difficult reading in the text." While this may be true in special cases, the typical variant footnote delivers only the most general information. In Matt 6:13, the note informs the reader that "some manuscripts add" the wording of the doxology.

Revised English Bible (REB)

The Revised English Bible (Oxford University Press, 1989), a revision of the New English Bible (1970), has, like its predecessor, enjoyed the support of the major church denominations of Great Britain, including the Roman Catholic Church. The preface to the REB informs the reader that

> where the Authorized [King James] Version contains passages which are found in the manuscripts on which that version rests, but which are absent from those followed by the Revised English Bible, these passages are reproduced in footnotes, in order to explain gaps in the verse numbering.

A separate introduction to the New Testament claims that there is "no scholarly Greek text of the New Testament which commands universal acceptance at the present time," yet the translators have used the twenty-sixth edition of the *NTG* as "a major point of reference" and have also taken into consideration the ongoing work of "exegetical and literary scholarship." To this end they have "drawn attention in footnotes to variant readings which may result in significant alternative understanding or interpretation of the text, and in particular to those readings which were followed in the New English Bible (NEB), but which now seem to the revisers to be less probable." In the case of Matt 6:13, the REB footnote, using its standard wording, simply points out that "Some witnesses add" the wording of the doxology, with no indication as to whether the footnote points to a variation from the KJV (as in this case) or the REB.

New King James Version (NKJV)

The New King James Version (Nelson, 1982) is essentially a modernization of the KJV, based on a similar Byzantine textual tradition. Predictably, then, the NKJV stands in the minority of contemporary translations in including the doxology in Matt 6:13. The preface indicates that the marginal notes point out, without making value judgments, significant places where the text differs from either the UBS/ eclectic tradition or the majority text tradition. The marginal footnote at Matt 6:13 indicates that the "NU text [this version's abbreviated reference to common text of the NA27/ UBS editions] omits *For Yours* through *Amen*."

Our survey of the manner in which some of the key contemporary English Bible translations handle textual variants brings both good news and bad news. On the positive side, all of the major translations surveyed provide in their footnotes helpful information about significant variants that occur in the Greek text that underlies the English translation. These footnotes provide readers with ready access to information about important variations in the New Testament textual tradition, allowing non-specialists to evaluate the alternate readings for themselves and to weigh them in the light of internal considerations such as context, style, and theological implications. On the negative side, the translations by and large give readers little or no means by which to evaluate variants other than the obvious fact that the translators have chosen to include one reading over the other(s) in their text. Thus the reader has no means by which to determine whether the evidence for the reading adopted by the translators is strong, or whether, as is often the case, the evidence for two or more readings is fairly evenly divided.

So what is the value of knowing that variants exist without being able to weigh the evidence for or against their authenticity? The question can be answered both in terms of internal and external evidence. In the first place, becoming aware of the variants reflected in one's English translation can provide the necessary impetus to weigh the intrinsic evidence for their authenticity (see chapter 7). Very often, by evaluating the variants as represented in English translations, one can employ the most basic tenet of textual criticism—seeking to determine which reading would more probably have given rise to the others. Other pieces of internal evidence, such as the relative brevity or difficulty of a particular reading, can also often be employed when considering variants in English translations.

Considering our example of the doxology of Matt 6:13, it isn't difficult to see how internal lines of evidence can fruitfully be applied even when dealing with the verse in an English translation. While it is easy, for example, to imagine how an existing liturgical formula might be (consciously or unconsciously) incorporated into the New Testament text, it is difficult to understand why a scribe might have deleted such a formulation if it were originally present. Also, since scribes typically tended to alter texts by filling them out, the MSS lacking the doxology have, on the basis of their brevity alone, some intrinsic likelihood of being authentic.

In the second place, one can at least make a broad evaluation of external evidence by comparing the texts and footnotes of various English translations. By placing the KJV or NKJV beside the NRSV or NIV, for example, one can perceive, in a general way, the differences between the Byzantine and Alexandrian-eclectic textual traditions, especially in places where those versions contain footnotes pointing to specific textual variants.[10]

Returning to our example of Matt 6:13, the NIV, following the critical eclectic text favored by most scholars, lacks the doxology. The NKJV, following the Byzantine text tradition considered by most contemporary textual scholars to represent, for the most part, a later, secondary, and edited form of the text, contains the doxology. Thus the external MS evidence, considered in the broadest sense, seems to corroborate the internal evidence just considered that the doxology should be regarded as a later addition to the text.

Other Textual Tools

Beyond the comparison of English translations, one can find a more detailed evaluation of the evidence for the more significant New Testament variants by using a textual commentary or a biblical commentary that includes discussions of textual questions. While textual commentaries can be quite technical and sometimes require some degree of facility in reading the New Testament text in the original Greek, they can also provide tremendous help in sorting through particular variants and in understanding the reasoning used by textual scholars in evaluating these variants. Bruce Metzger's widely used *A Textual Commentary on the Greek New Testament* discusses the major variants of the UBS4 edition, shedding light on how the UBS Editorial Committee came to the conclusions it did regarding each reading. Each variant chosen for inclusion in the UBS text is also assigned a grade from A to D showing the level of confidence the committee had in the chosen variant's authenticity. Because Metzger's *Textual Commentary* often discusses variants by referring to the original Greek and using technical language and concepts, it may prove challenging for the non-specialist. A more accessible work is Roger L. Omanson's *A Textual Guide to the Greek New Testament,* which is an adaptation of Metzger's *Textual Commentary.* Omanson's guide, created specifically for use by Bible translators who may lack extensive training in textual criticism, provides readers with a relatively non-technical discussion of the most significant New Testament variants.

Omanson's entry for Matt 6:13 presents the evidence for ending the Lord's Prayer with the Greek word πονηροῦ (*ponērou*):

6.13 πονηροῦ. (the Evil one/evil.) {A}

Early and important manuscripts of the Alexandrian, Western, and other types of text, as well as commentaries on the Lord's Prayer by early Church Fathers, end the Lord's Prayer with the word πονηροῦ in v. 13. Copyists added several different endings in order to adapt the Prayer for use in worship in the early church. Additions include the following: (a) "for yours is the kingdom, and the power, and the glory forever. Amen" (so Seg); (b) "for yours is the kingdom and the glory forever. Amen"; and (c) "for yours is the kingdom and the power and the glory of the Father and of the Son and of the Holy Spirit forever. Amen."[11]

Omanson's adaptation of Metzger's commentary avoids technical text-critical language and is sparse in its use of Greek. Note that the reading adopted in the text (lacking the doxology) is given the grade of {A}, showing a high level of confidence that the original text of the New Testament did not include the language. Omanson then provides a general summary of the evidence for the shorter reading, which includes Alexandrian, Western, and other types of text. He concludes by listing several variants involving additions to the text, including the standard Byzantine doxology, which, he reasons (following Metzger and the UBS Editorial Committee), were added "to adapt the Prayer for use in worship in the early church."

In the NET Bible's text-critical note for Matt 6:13, the doxology, which is omitted from the text, is helpfully cited both in Greek and in English. The evidence for and against the inclusion of the doxology is cited in terms of specific manuscripts, versions, and church fathers. The witnesses cited amount to a digest of information derived from the critical apparatus of the NA27, and there is no discussion of text-types as they relate to the variant in question. The editors conclude that the omission of the doxology is attested by "better witnesses," but those without special training in textual criticism will have some difficulty evaluating the external evidence for themselves. Non-specialists will find the discussion of the probable origins of the doxology more helpful. With Metzger, whose *Textual Commentary* (TCGNT) is explicitly cited, the NET Bible editors surmise that the doxology arose in a context of early Christian worship.

Certain scholarly New Testament commentaries provide yet another helpful source of information related to New Testament textual variants. Many New Testament commentaries brush over issues of textual criticism or defer to the judgment of critical editions of the New Testament or textual commentaries. However, a few noteworthy commentary series include within their stated purpose the discussion of text-critical issues. Among these are the Hermeneia (Augsburg), the International Critical Commentary (ICC; T&T Clark), and the Word Biblical Commentary (WBC; Word) series. Readers should be aware that since the commentaries that include text-critical discussions tend to be designed for biblical scholars, the discussion may at times deal with the text using the original languages or other kinds of technical language that may present a challenge to the non-specialist.

In summary, with the exception of the NKJV and a few other KJV-based translations, contemporary English versions of the New Testament tend to be based on an Alexandrian-eclectic form of the Greek text similar to that of the NA/UBS text. Yet for the most part, these current translations include footnotes that highlight key variants within the New Testament textual tradition, including those from the Byzantine tradition. These footnotes can provide information that readers of the English Bible can use in weighing the internal evidence for particular readings. A broad comparison of most modern versions with the NKJV can reveal where the Alexandrian-eclectic text varies from the Byzantine text-type. Additional textual helps such as textual or critical commentaries can provide reasoned arguments related to variants and can assist readers in assessing the degree of likelihood for one reading over against another.

CHAPTER TEN

What Shall We Say to These Things?

What conclusions can we draw from all that we have said? How should we look upon the text of the New Testament as it is reflected in the Greek text available to us today as well as in the common English versions that are being read?

In these pages we have seen that the great majority of textual differences between the MSS are matters of small details that have no real theological significance. To underscore this fact, I would cite the following list of variants in addition to those we have already looked at:

Mark 8:26—"Don't even go into the village" / "Don't tell it to anyone in the village" / "Don't even go into the village nor tell it to anyone in the village" / "Go into your house and don't tell it to anyone in the village" / "Go into your house and if you go into the village don't tell it to anyone, not even in the village" / "Go into your house and if you go into the village don't tell it to anyone" / "Go into your house and don't even go into the village nor tell it to anyone in the village" / "And if you go into the village don't tell it to anyone in the village"

John 5:17—"but he [the context obviously indicating Jesus] answered them" / "but Jesus answered them"

Acts 2:24—"the pains of death" / "the pains of Hades"

Phil 1:14—"to speak the word" / "to speak the word of God"

1 Thess 2:15—"who killed both the Lord Jesus and the prophets" / "who killed both the Lord Jesus and their own prophets"

2 Thess 2:8—"whom the Lord will destroy" / "whom the Lord Jesus will destroy"

2 Tim 2:14—"before God" / "before the Lord"

Titus 1:10—"many who are insubordinate" / "many who are also insubordinate"

The list could be extended for longer than anyone would care to read. I present it for a specific reason. There are those who insist that some of the MSS most scholars consider reliable have in fact been intentionally corrupted to omit or weaken important doctrines of the Christian faith.

I offer three points in rebuttal to this claim:

1. As we have just noted, by far the most variants have no theological significance at all. Furthermore, the vast majority of the most theologically significant passages of the New Testament have no significant textual variations. Among the few variants that do have theological significance, scribes have sometimes apparently attempted to move the text in an orthodox rather than a heretical direction. But regardless of the motivation of the scribes, the small number of intentional variants that exist do not stand up under the scrutiny of the internal and external evidence.

2. The Greek MSS of the New Testament widely recognized to be valid do not in any way consistently weaken, pervert, or omit any theological point or doctrine. On the contrary, MSS that critics condemn for omitting or changing a supposedly significant word or phrase in one passage will invariably be seen to contain the same word or idea in other

passages. If the variant indicates an attempt to corrupt the text, why did the scribe content himself with corrupting it in one passage but not in other passages?

3. It is not without significance that the very MSS or texts that these critics acclaim as the true and faithful texts are occasionally guilty of the very type of variant they call heresy in other texts. For example, it is the Byzantine text-type and the Textus Receptus that in 1 John 3:1 omit the strong words "and we are [children of God]." Just a few verses earlier, in 1 John 2:23, it is again the Byzantine text and the Textus Receptus that omit the entire clause "he who confesses the Son has the Father also." Such omissions are precisely the sort of thing such critics are inclined to decry as heresy elsewhere.

The truth, of course, is that such charges of deliberate corruption are false. Let us remind ourselves again that scribes were engaged in copying the text, not in studying it, when they did their work. Indeed, many textual errors arose from the very fact that the scribe was not thinking of the meaning or the full sense of the passage he was copying.

To get an idea of the sort of arguments that are sometimes used, it may be worth referring to some notes I received from a message given by a well-known clergyman from Northern Ireland. In this message he attacked the New International Version of the New Testament specifically, but his charges were actually directed against the Greek text from which this English version was translated, which is essentially the text I have been supporting in this book and which most recent versions follow. Among his comments were the following:

Matthew 1:25—Because the NIV follows the Greek reading "until she gave birth to a son" instead of the KJV's "till she had brought forth her firstborn son," this clergyman charged the NIV with "striking at the virgin birth of Christ"! In actual fact, of course, the variant has nothing whatever to do with the question of the virgin birth, and the criticism is sheer rabble-rousing. Indeed, since this particular clergyman is violently anti–Roman Catholic, he could more logically (but still fallaciously) have seen the NIV reading as an accommodation to the Roman Catholic doctrine that Mary had no more children after the birth of Jesus!

Luke 2:33—Because the NIV reads, "the child's father and mother marveled," where the KJV reads, "Joseph and his mother marveled," this clergyman charges that the NIV implies that Joseph was the father of Jesus, thus denying the virgin birth. He conveniently overlooks Luke 2:48, only a few lines farther on, in which the KJV and all other versions quote Mary herself as saying to Jesus that *"your father and I have been anxiously searching for you"*!

Matthew 25:13—He charges that by reading, "Therefore keep watch, because you do not know the day or the hour," and omitting the addition found in the KJV, "wherein the Son of man cometh," the NIV is "striking at the second coming of Christ." This is patently a false accusation. This sort of reference to the "day" and the "hour" clearly implies the return of Christ. More than this, the whole context from the beginning of chapter 24 bespeaks the second coming of Christ.

Charges such as these must be ascribed to ignorance, willful prejudice, or both.

Differences Other than Variants

It is important to remember that not all differences mentioned in our common English versions arise from differences between ancient MSS; many result from different interpretations of the same Greek word or phrase into English. To signal these different possibilities, both the NRSV and the NIV include footnotes consisting of the word "Or" followed by the alternate interpretation. For example, in John 2:23 the NIV text reads, "believed in his name," and the footnote reads, "Or *and believed in him.*" In John 3:3 the text of the NRSV reads, "born from above," and the footnote reads, "Or *born anew.*" If the difference is a textual variant, on the other hand, the footnote will state, "Other ancient authorities read," "Some early MSS read," or something similar. For example, in Luke 22:16 the NRSV text reads, "not eat it," and the footnote reads, "Other ancient authorities read *never eat it again.*"

And Finally . . .

What can we conclude from our study of the MSS of the New Testament as they were copied and handed down through these nearly two thousand years?

We see that the inspired New Testament text was a Greek text and that any translation can be considered to be the word of God only insofar as it presents the message that was given by the original authors in Greek. Only they, and no later scribes, editors, or translators, were given the unique inspiration of the Holy Spirit to put God's revelation into human words.

We see that in the thousands of MSS of the New Testament that were copied through the centuries and the millions of words they contain there are countless differences of words, word order, and word forms. Yet the evidence is clear that most of these differences are accidental or insignificant and that when scribes intentionally changed a text, they usually did so to clarify or strengthen the meaning; there is virtually no evidence of a scribe intentionally trying to weaken or corrupt the text. We have seen, in addition, that by use of established and reasonable principles we can decide between variants in most instances and determine which is the original reading.

Finally, and very importantly, we see that we do not have to close our minds to the history of the New Testament text in order to prevent our confidence in the New Testament as we have it from being weakened or destroyed. Rather, we can be certain that God has preserved his word down through the centuries. Sir Frederic Kenyon, one of the greatest and most respected scholars of New Testament MSS of the past century, expresses this conviction well when he closes his book *The Story of the Bible* with these words: "It is reassuring at the end to find that the general result of all these discoveries and all this study is to strengthen the proof of the authenticity of the Scriptures, and our conviction that we have in our hands, in substantial integrity, the veritable Word of God."[12]

Notes

1. Perhaps the best known recent example of this line of argumentation is Bart Ehrman's *Misquoting Jesus: The Story Behind Who Changed the Bible and Why* (San Francisco: HarperSanFrancisco, 2005). For a balanced critique of Ehrman's book, see Daniel Wallace, "The Gospel According to Bart: A Review Article of *Misquoting Jesus* by Bart Ehrman," *Journal of the Evangelical Theological Society*, 49:2 (June 2006): 327–49.

2. See Bruce M. Metzger, *The Text of the New Testament: Its Transmission, Corruption, and Restoration* (Oxford: Oxford University Press, 1992), 158.

3. B. F. Westcott and F. J. A. Hort, *The Greek New Testament* (Peabody, Mass.: Hendrickson, 2007), 888.

4. Ibid., 887.

5. Ibid., 888.

6. The translation is that of Bruce Metzger, *A Textual Commentary on the Greek New Testament* (2d ed.; New York: United Bible Societies, 2005), 117.

7. The text of the third edition of the UBS *GNT* is virtually identical to that of the fourth edition.

8. Introduction to the First Edition, p. 24.

9. The texts of the two Greek editions are, apart from minor punctuation differences, virtually identical.

10. This can most readily be done by using a Bible that contains a number of parallel versions in side-by-side columns, such as the *Hendrickson Parallel Bible* (Peabody, Mass.: Hendrickson, 2008).

11. Roger L. Omanson, *A Textual Guide to the Greek New Testament* (Stuttgart: German Bible Society, 2006), 8.

12. Sir Frederic Kenyon, *The Story of the Bible* (2d ed.; London: John Murray, 1964), 113.

Bibliography

Aland, Kurt, and Barbara Aland. *The Text of the New Testament: An Introduction to the Critical Editions and to the Theory and Practice of Modern Textual Criticism.* Grand Rapids: Eerdmans, 1995.

Black, David Alan. *New Testament Textual Criticism: A Concise Guide.* Grand Rapids: Baker, 1994.

Bruce, F. F. *The New Testament Documents: Are They Reliable?* 6th ed. Grand Rapids: Eerdmans; Downers Grove, Ill.: InterVarsity, 1981.

Comfort, Philip Wesley. *Encountering the Manuscripts: An Introduction to New Testament Paleography & Textual Criticism.* Nashville: Broadman & Holman, 2005.

Epp, Eldon Jay. *Perspectives on New Testament Textual Criticism: Collected Essays, 1962–2004.* Supplements to *Novum Testamentum.* Leiden: E. J. Brill, 2005.

Epp, Eldon Jay, and Gordon D. Fee. *Studies in the Theory and Method of New Testament Textual Criticism.* Grand Rapids: Eerdmans, 1993.

Greenlee, J. Harold. *Introduction to New Testament Textual Criticism.* Rev. ed. Peabody, Mass.: Hendrickson, 1995.

Metzger, Bruce M. *A Textual Commentary on the Greek New Testament.* 2d ed. New York: United Bible Societies, 2005.

Metzger, Bruce M., and Bart D. Ehrman. *The Text of the New Testament: Its Transmission, Corruption, and Restoration.* 4th ed. New York: Oxford University Press, 2005.

Omanson, Roger L. *Textual Guide to the Greek New Testament: An Adaptation of B. Metzger's Textual Commentary.* Stuttgart: German Bible Society, 2006.

Wegner, Paul D. *A Student's Guide to Textual Criticism of the Bible: Its History, Methods and Results.* Downers Grove, Ill.: InterVarsity, 2006.

Index of People and Subjects

Aland, Kurt, 55
Alexandrian text-type (MSS), 70–71, 82, 85, 90, 96, 105
Alexandrinus. *See under* codex
American Bible Society, 55
Ammonian Sections, 101
apparatus, critical, 50–51, 53–56, 114
Armenian. *See under* versions
autograph(s), 2, 15, 21, 33, 76, 103, 105

Bengel, J. A., 49–50, 51, 76
Bezae. *See under* codex
biblos, biblion, 8, 9, 13
Bodmer Library, 15, 24
Bohairic. *See* versions
book. *See* codex
Byzantine text, 42, 70, 73–74, 84, 93, 94, 96–97, 100–101, 104–9, 112, 115, 118. *See also* Textus Receptus

Caesarean text-type, 41, 69
Cardinal's edition, 44
Challoner, Bishop, 106
chapter divisions, 47
Chester Beatty Library, 17, 22

church fathers, 27, 34, 50–51, 58, 74, 100–101, 109, 113, 114. *See also* patristic quotations
Claromontanus. *See under* codex
codex, 14–17
   Aleph (‭א‬), 26, 74, 95
   Alexandrinus (A), 25–26
   Bezae (D), 25, 26, 27, 74, 87–88
   Claromontanus (D), 26, 27, 87–88
   Codex 33, 28, 51, 74
   Codex 61, 46
   Codex C, 53
   Codex Vaticanus (B), 17, 27, 30, 55, 56, 74, 101
   Ephraemi Rescriptus, 53
   Petropolitanus, 27
   Sinaiticus (‭א‬), 17, 25, 26, 27, 28, 30, 53, 54, 56, 74, 101
   Theta (Θ), 74
   Washingtoniensis (W), 74
   Zacynthius, 27
commentary, biblical, 113, 115
Complutensian Polyglot, 44, 46–47
Constantine, 24, 41
Constantinople, 35
contractions, 20

UBS. *See* United Bible Societies
Ulfilas, Bishop, 33
United Bible Societies, editorial committee, 56, 106, 113–14
United Bible Societies (UBS) Greek New Testament, 55
3d edition, 56
4th edition, 56
uncial. *See* handwriting, types of uncial manuscripts. *See under* manuscripts

variants: nature of, 48, 75, 79–82, 84, 94–97, 117
number of, 39–40, 51, 58, 68, 75
ranking of, 38–39, 55–56, 77, 83, 87–106
summary of, 37–38, 39, 55, 71, 111–17
Vaticanus. *See under* codex
vellum, 10
verse divisions in New Testament, 46, 101
versions, 29–33
Armenian, 33, 74

Bohairic, 33, 74
Coptic, 33
Latin, 3, 27, 31–32, 42, 44–46, 78, 105–6
Old Latin, 74
others, 33
Syriac, 32–34, 65, 74
Vulgate, Latin, 31–32, 35, 42, 44, 46, 78, 80, 105–6

Westcott, Brooke Foss, 54–56, 76, 105
Westcott/Hort Greek New Testament, 54, 76, 105
Western church, 105
Western text, 70, 105–7
Wetstein, J. J., 51
Weymouth Greek New Testament, 55
word of God, 4, 36, 56, 117, 120
writing implements, 11–12

Ximenes, Cardinal, 44–45

Zacynthius. *See under* codex

Index of Biblical References

Romans
4:19   92
5:1   72
15:30   79
16:22   21

1 Corinthians
6:12–20   98
6:20   98
6:21   22
7:5   97
8:6   80
11:29   89
12:9–11   77
13:3   66
16:21   22

2 Corinthians
3:17   80
13:14   79

Galatians
4:7   91
6:11   22

Ephesians
1:1   88
1:7   61

Philippians
1:1   88
1:14   117

Colossians
1:14   61
1:20   61
2:2   91
4:18   22

1 Thessalonians
2:7   64
2:15   114

2 Thessalonians
2:3   85
2:8   117
3:17   21

1 Timothy
3:16   65

2 Timothy
2:14   117
4:13   14

Titus
1:10   117

1 Peter
1:2   65, 79

2 Peter
1:21   37

1 John
1:4   66
2:23   64, 118, 119
3:1   93, 118
4:20   94
5:7–8   78

2 John
12   8, 12

3 John
13   11–12

Jude
20–21   79–80

Revelation
1:5   66
5:1   9
6:14   14
12:18   89